YOUR PERSONAL

ASTROLOGY

PLANNER

GEMINI
2011

YOUR PERSONAL
ASTROLOGY
PLANNER

GEMINI
2011

RICK LEVINE **& JEFF** JAWER

STERLING

New York / London
www.sterlingpublishing.com

STERLING and the distinctive Sterling logo are registered trademarks of
Sterling Publishing Co., Inc.

2 4 6 8 10 9 7 5 3 1

Published by Sterling Publishing Co., Inc.
387 Park Avenue South, New York, NY 10016
© 2010 Sterling Publishing Co., Inc.
Text © 2010 Rick Levine and Jeff Jawer
Distributed in Canada by Sterling Publishing
C/o Canadian Manda Group, 165 Dufferin Street,
Toronto, Ontario, Canada M6K 3H6
Distributed in the United Kingdom by GMC Distribution Services
Castle Place, 166 High Street, Lewes, East Sussex, England BN7 1XU
Distributed in Australia by Capricorn Link (Australia) Pty. Ltd.
P.O. Box 704, Windsor, NSW 2756, Australia

Printed in Canada
All rights reserved

Sterling ISBN 978-1-4027-7475-1

For information about custom editions, special sales, premium and
corporate purchases, please contact Sterling Special Sales
Department at 800-805-5489 or specialsales@sterlingpublishing.com.

TABLE OF CONTENTS

THE PURPOSE OF THIS BOOK

The more you learn about yourself, the better able you are to wisely use the energies in your life.
For more than 3,000 years, astrology has been the sharpest tool in the box for describing the human condition. Used by virtually every culture on the planet, astrology continues to serve as a link between individual lives and planetary cycles. We gain valuable insights into personal issues with a birth chart, and can plot the patterns of the year ahead in meaningful ways for individuals as well as groups. You share your sun sign with eight percent of humanity. Clearly, you're not all going to have the same day, even if the basic astrological cycles are the same. Your individual circumstances, the specific factors of your entire birth chart, and your own free will help you write your unique story.

The purpose of this book is to describe the energies of the Sun, Moon, and planets for the year ahead and help you create your future, rather than being a victim of it. We aim to facilitate your journey by showing you the turns ahead in the road of life and hopefully the best ways to navigate them.

YOU ARE THE STAR OF YOUR LIFE

It is not our goal to simply predict events. Rather, we are reporting the planetary energies—the cosmic weather in which you are living—so that you understand these conditions and know how to use them most effectively.

The power, though, isn't in the stars, but in your mind, your heart, and the choices that you make every day. Regardless of how strongly you are buffeted by the winds of change or bored by stagnation, you have many ways to view any situation. Learning about the energies of the Sun, Moon, and planets will both sharpen and widen your perspective, thereby giving you additional choices.

The language of astrology is a gift of awareness, not a rigid set of rules. It works best when blended with common sense, intuition, and self-trust. This is your life, and no one knows how to live it as well as you. Take what you need from this book and leave the rest. Although the planets set the stage for the year ahead, you're the writer, director, and star of your life and you can play the part in whatever way you choose. *Your Personal Astrology Planner* uses information about your sun sign to give you a better understanding of how the planetary waves will wash upon your shore. We each navigate our lives through time, and each moment has unique qualities. Astrology gives us the ability to describe the constantly changing timescape. For example, if you know the trajectory and the speed of an approaching storm, you can choose to delay a leisurely afternoon sail on the bay, thus avoiding an unpleasant situation.

By reading this book, you can improve your ability to align with the cosmic weather, the larger patterns that affect you day to day. You can become more effective by aligning with the cosmos and cocreating the year ahead with a better understanding of the energies around you.

Astrology doesn't provide quick fixes to life's complex issues. It doesn't offer neatly packed black-and-white answers in a world filled with an infinite variety of shapes and colors. It can, however, give you a much clearer picture of the invisible forces influencing your life.

ENERGY & EVENTS

Two sailboats can face the same gale yet travel in opposite directions as a result of how the sails are positioned. Similarly, how you respond to the energy of a particular set of circumstances may be more responsible for your fate than the given situation itself. We delineate the energetic winds for your year ahead, but your attitude shapes the unfolding events, and your responses alter your destiny.

This book emphasizes the positive, not because all is good, but because astrology shows us ways to transform even the power of a storm into beneficial results. Empowerment comes from learning to see the invisible energy patterns that impact the visible landscape as you fill in the details of your story every day on this spinning planet, orbited by the Moon, lit by the Sun, and colored by the nuances of the planets.

You are a unique point in an infinite galaxy of unlimited possibilities, and the choices that you make have consequences. So use this book in a most magical way to consciously improve your life.

MOON CHARTS

2011 NEW MOONS

Each New Moon marks the beginning of a cycle. In general, this is the best time to plant seeds for future growth. Use the days preceeding the New Moon to finish old business prior to starting what comes next. The focused mind can be quite sharp during this phase. Harness the potential of the New Moon by stating your intentions—out loud or in writing—for the weeks ahead. Hold these goals in your mind and help them grow to fruition through conscious actions as the Moon gains light during the following two weeks. In the chart below, the dates and times refer to when the Moon and Sun align in each zodiac sign (see p16), initiating a new lunar cycle.

DATE	TIME	SIGN
January 4	4:03 am EST	Capricorn (ECLIPSE)
February 2	9:31 pm EST	Aquarius
March 4	3:46 pm EST	Pisces
April 3	10:32 am EDT	Aries
May 3	2:51 am EDT	Taurus
June 1	5:03 pm EDT	Gemini (ECLIPSE)
July 1	4:54 am EDT	Cancer (ECLIPSE)
July 30	2:40 pm EDT	Leo
August 28	11:04 pm EDT	Virgo
September 27	7:09 pm EDT	Libra
October 26	3:56 pm EDT	Scorpio
November 25	1:10 am EST	Sagittarius (ECLIPSE)
December 24	1:06 pm EST	Capricorn

2011 FULL MOONS

The Full Moon reflects the light of the Sun as sub-
jective feelings reflect the objective events of the
day. Dreams seem bigger; moods feel stronger. The
emotional waters run with deeper currents. This
is the phase of culmination, a turning point in the
energetic cycle. Now it's time to listen to the inner
voices. Rather than starting new projects,
the two weeks after the Full Moon are when we
complete what we can and slow our outward
expressions in anticipation of the next New Moon.
In this chart, the dates and times refer to when
the moon is opposite the sun in each zodiac sign,
marking the emotional peak of each lunar cycle.

DATE	TIME	SIGN
January 19	4:21 pm EST	Cancer
February 18	3:35 am EST	Leo
March 19	2:10 pm EDT	Virgo
April 17	10:44 pm EDT	Libra
May 17	7:09 am EDT	Scorpio
June 15	4:14 pm EDT	Sagittarius (ECLIPSE)
July 15	2:40 am EDT	Capricorn
August 13	2:57 pm EDT	Aquarius
September 12	5:27 am EDT	Pisces
October 11	10:06 pm EDT	Aries
November 10	3:16 pm EST	Taurus
December 10	9:36 am EST	Gemini (ECLIPSE)

ASTROLOGY, YOU & THE WORLD

WELCOME TO YOUR SUN SIGN

The Sun, Moon, and Earth and all the planets lie within a plane called the **ecliptic** and move through a narrow band of stars made up by 12 constellations called the **zodiac**. The Earth revolves around the Sun once a year, but from our point of view, it appears that the Sun moves through each sign of the zodiac for one month. There are 12 months and astrologically there are 12 signs. The astrological months, however, do not match our calendar, and start between the 19th and 23rd of each month. Everyone is born to an astrological month, like being born in a room with a particular perspective of the world. Knowing your sun sign provides useful information about your personality and your future, but for a more detailed astrological analysis, a full birth chart calculation based on your precise date, time, and place of birth is necessary. Get your complete birth chart online at:

http://www.tarot.com/astrology/astroprofile

This book is about your zodiac sign. Your Sun is in the air sign of curious Gemini, the Twins. For you, life presents itself as a spectrum of possibilities, and you tune in to and out of experiences as if you were listening to a radio. Duality is your theme; there is always an alternate station. At your worst, you might be scattered, but your greatest strengths are your active mind, your cleverness with words, and the ability to think on your feet.

THE PLANETS

We refer to the Sun and Moon as planets. Don't worry; we do know about modern astronomy. Although the Sun is really a star and the Moon is a satellite, they are called planets for astrological purposes. The astrological planets are the Sun, the Moon, Mercury, Venus, Mars, Jupiter, Saturn, Chiron, Uranus, Neptune, and Pluto.

Your sun sign is the most obvious astrological placement, for the Sun returns to the same sign every year. But at the same time, the Moon is orbiting the Earth, changing signs every two and a third days. Mercury, Venus, and Mars each move through a sign in a few weeks to a few months.

Jupiter spends a whole year in a sign—and Pluto visits a sign for up to 30 years! The ever-changing positions of the planets alter the energetic terrain through which we travel. The planets are symbols; each has a particular range of meanings. For example, Venus is the goddess of love, but it really symbolizes beauty in a spectrum of experiences. Venus can represent romantic love, sensuality, the arts, or good food. It activates anything that we value, including personal possessions and even money. To our ancestors, the planets actually animated life on Earth. In this way of thinking, every beautiful flower contains the essence of Venus.

Each sign has a natural affinity to an individual planet, and as this planet moves through the sky, it sends messages of particular interest to people born under that sign. Your key or ruling planet is Mercury, the Messenger of the Heavens. Quicksilver Mercury is the fastest of the true planets, symbolic of the speed and changeability of thought. Its function is to send and receive data through all forms of intelligible communication. Its movement shows the qualities of your thinking process and speech. Planets can be described by many different words, for the mythology of each is a rich tapestry. In this book we use a variety of words when talking about each planet in order to convey the most applicable meaning. The table below describes a few keywords for each planet, including the Sun and Moon.

PLANET	SYMBOL	KEYWORDS
Sun	☉	Consciousness, Will, Vitality
Moon	☽	Subconscious, Emotions, Habits
Mercury	☿	Communication, Thoughts, Transportation
Venus	♀	Desire, Love, Money, Values
Mars	♂	Action, Physical Energy, Drive
Jupiter	♃	Expansion, Growth, Optimism
Saturn	♄	Contraction, Maturity, Responsibility
Chiron	⚷	Healing, Pain, Subversion
Uranus	♅	Awakening, Unpredictable, Inventive
Neptune	♆	Imagination, Spirituality, Confusion
Pluto	♇	Passion, Intensity, Regeneration

HOUSES

Just as planets move through the signs of the zodiac, they also move through the houses in an individual chart. The 12 houses correspond to the 12 signs, but are individualized, based upon your sign. In this book we use Solar Houses, which place your sun sign in your 1st House. Therefore, when a planet enters a new sign it also enters a new house. If you know your exact time of birth, the rising sign determines the 1st House. You can learn your rising sign by entering your birth date at:

http://www.tarot.com/astrology/astroprofile

HOUSE	SIGN	KEYWORDS
1st House	Aries	Self, Appearance, Personality
2nd House	Taurus	Possessions, Values, Self-Worth
3rd House	Gemini	Communication, Siblings, Short Trips
4th House	Cancer	Home, Family, Roots
5th House	Leo	Love, Romance, Children, Play
6th House	Virgo	Work, Health, Daily Routines
7th House	Libra	Marriage, Relationships, Business Partners
8th House	Scorpio	Intimacy, Transformation, Shared Resources
9th House	Sagittarius	Travel, Higher Education, Philosophy
10th House	Capricorn	Career, Community, Ambition
11th House	Aquarius	Groups and Friends, Associations, Social Ideals
12th House	Pisces	Imagination, Spirituality, Secret Activities

ASPECTS

As the planets move through the sky in their various cycles, they form ever-changing angles with one another. Certain angles create signifi-cant geometric shapes. So, when two planets are 90 degrees apart, they conform to a square; 60 degrees of separation conforms to a sextile, or six-pointed star. Planets create **aspects** when they're at these special angles. Aspects explain how the individual symbolism of pairs of planets combine into an energetic pattern.

ASPECT	DEGREES	KEYWORD
Conjunction	0	Compression, Blending, Focus
Opposition	180	Tension, Awareness, Balance
Trine	120	Harmony, Free-Flowing, Ease
Square	90	Resistance, Stress, Dynamic Conflict
Quintile	72	Creativity, Metaphysical, Magic
Sextile	60	Support, Intelligent, Activating
Quincunx	150	Irritation, Annoyance, Adjustment

2011 GENERAL FORECAST

Astrology works for individuals, groups, and humanity as a whole. You will have your own story in 2011, but it will unfold among nearly seven billion other tales of human experience. We are each unique, yet our lives touch one another; our destinies are woven together by weather and war, by the economy, science, music, politics, religion, and all the other threads of life on planet Earth.

This astrological look at the major trends and planetary patterns for 2011 provides a framework for comprehending the potentials and challenges we face together, so that we can move forward with tolerance and respect as a community as we also fulfill our potential as individuals.

The astrological events used for this forecast are the transits of major planets Jupiter and Saturn, the retrograde cycles of Mercury, and the Eclipses of the Sun and the Moon.

A NOTE ABOUT DATES IN THIS BOOK

All events are based upon the Eastern Time Zone of the United States. Because of local time differences, an event occurring just a few minutes after midnight in the East will actually happen the prior day in the rest of the country. Although the key dates are the exact dates of any particular alignment, some of you are so ready for certain things to happen that you can react to a transit a day or two before it is exact. And sometimes you can be so entrenched in habits or unwilling to change that you may not notice the effects right away. Allow extra time around each key date to feel the impact of any event.

JUPITER IN PISCES:
INTO THE MYSTIC
January 17, 2010–June 6, 2010
September 9, 2010–January 22, 2011

Jupiter, the planet of expansion, reconnects us with our spiritual roots in its traditional home sign of Pisces. Knowledge is no longer an intellectual abstraction; it's a living experience that comes from our emotional connection to the cosmos. Imagination is stronger now as the limits of logic are dissolved in the boundless waters of intuition that can reveal answers to all of life's questions.

We can grasp complex concepts and subtle metaphysical truths without having to put them into words, yet we can use art, poetry, music, and dance to express them eloquently. Jupiter in Pisces brings the gift of wisdom that is equally available to all.

JUPITER IN ARIES:
BRAVE NEW WORLD
June 6, 2010–September 9, 2010
January 22, 2011–June 4, 2011

A new day dawns with farseeing Jupiter in pioneering Aries. The urge to test ideas on the battlefield of experience amplifies impatience yet rewards individuals and institutions willing to take risks. Breakthroughs in energy generation are now possible. Innovations in education and travel are likely to follow. However, failure to compromise on ideological matters can increase the potential for conflict. Bold statements and actions provoke rapid responses, reducing the effectiveness of diplomacy. New ways of seeing ourselves can quickly break down old barriers, allowing our common humanity to overcome differences of nationality, ideology, religion, and race. We may finally be ready for the future, able to address immediate crises with modern ideas to lead us into a desirable tomorrow rather than recycling tired beliefs from the past. Leaping into action without carefully considering the consequences can lead to mistakes, but the benefits gained by this kind of spontaneity will more than compensate for any losses.

JUPITER IN TAURUS:
EARTHLY PURSUITS
June 4, 2011–June 11, 2012

Now that new visions have been sparked by Jupiter in fiery Aries, it's time to turn these innovations into enduring systems. Bright ideas come down to earth in practical Taurus, where we can gain material benefits from recent discoveries. Viable sources of cheaper and cleaner energy reflect the gifts of generous Jupiter in this resource-rich sign. However, we may be more stubborn and resistant to unfamiliar ideas now. A selfish desire for wealth can close minds to inspiring concepts that lack immediate practical application. Philosophical Jupiter in fixed Taurus narrows our intellectual comfort zone, so we don't ask provocative questions that challenge our core beliefs. It can also decrease our interest in any opportunity unless we're assured of practical results.

SATURN IN LIBRA:
LIVES IN THE BALANCE
October 29, 2009–April 7, 2010
July 21, 2010–October 5, 2012

Saturn's shift into peace-loving Libra marked a new chapter in all of our relationships, but we still have some tough work to do before we can achieve the harmony it promises. When Saturn in Libra functions at its best, cooperation and civility allow diplomacy to flourish as reason replaces force. The need to weigh both sides of any argument can slow personal and public dialogue, yet it's worth the price to build bridges over seemingly impassable chasms. Saturn is "exalted" in Libra according to astrological tradition, suggesting a highly positive link between the planet's principle of integrity and Libra's sense of fair play. The negative side of Saturn, though, is its potential for rigidity, which can manifest now as a stubborn unwillingness to listen. Resistance to opposing points of view is simply an opportunity to test their worth; only with careful consideration can they be properly evaluated.

Karmic Saturn is judgmental and known to deliver exactly what we deserve. When in Libra the Scales, justice becomes one way of restoring balance. Accordingly, we will continue to see legal systems around the world taking steps to correct social inequities and governmental and corporate abuses of power. In the United States, we will see ongoing political attempts to establish harmony between historically divided camps with polarized views about individual rights on such fundamental issues as abortion and euthanasia. The courts will be expected to adjudicate these differences, even when there seems to be no common ground. Since Libra is the sign of relationships, we can also expect more cases that address the spreading acceptance of same-sex marriage.

MERCURY RETROGRADES
March 30–April 23 in Aries /
August 2 in Virgo, Direct August 26 in Leo /
November 24–December 13 in Sagittarius

All true planets appear to move backward from time to time, because we view them from the moving platform of Earth. The most noticeable and regular retrograde periods are those of Mercury, the communication planet. Occurring three or four times a year for roughly three weeks at a time, these are times when difficulties with details, travel, communication, and technical matters seem more common than usual.

Although many people think that Mercury's retrograde is negative, you can make this cycle work for you. Because personal and commercial interactions are emphasized, you can actually accomplish more than usual, especially if you stay focused on what you need to do rather than initiating new projects. Still, you may feel as if you're treading water—or worse, being carried backward in an undertow of unfinished business. Worry less about making progress than about the quality of your work. Pay extra attention to all your communication exchanges. Avoiding misunderstandings and omissions is the ideal way to minimize complications. Retrograde Mercury is best used to tie up loose ends as you review, redo, reconsider, and, in general, revisit the past.

ECLIPSES
Solar: January 4, June 1, July 1, and November 25
Lunar: June 15 and December 10

Solar and Lunar Eclipses are special New and Full Moons that indicate significant changes for individuals and groups. They are powerful markers of events with influences that can appear up to three months in advance and last up to six months afterward.

January 4, Solar Eclipse in Capricorn: Question Authority
This Solar Eclipse in authoritative Capricorn represents a potential loss of status. Aggressive Mars's conjunction with the Sun and Moon indicates challenges to a person's position, especially for leaders of nations on the eclipse path that runs through northern Africa, Europe, and eastern Asia. Strict Saturn's square to the eclipse demands discipline and could slow or even stop the advance of overly ambitious individuals.

June 1, Solar Eclipse in Gemini: Lighten Up
Although this Solar Eclipse is in jittery Gemini and joined with the draining South Node of the

Moon, it's more like a gentle shakeup than a major breakdown thanks to a supportive trine from Saturn. It is a reminder to set new priorities and eliminate inessential activities. Its visibility in eastern Russia, Alaska, northern Canada, and Greenland makes these prime regions for change.

June 15, Lunar Eclipse in Sagittarius:
Free Your Mind
This Lunar Eclipse in open-minded Sagittarius could clip the wings of religious leaders, reshape laws, and improve legal systems. It signals a step back from orthodoxy and a willingness to engage in dialogue with individuals of differing points of view. Mental Mercury is joined with the Sun in clever Gemini, raising the stakes in a debate. Conversation and conviviality are worth more now than the claim of absolute truth.

July 1, Solar Eclipse in Cancer:
Sink or Swim
This Solar Eclipse in tribal and nationalistic Cancer is opposed by powerful Pluto and squared by unpredictable Uranus. Unfortunately, the energy could be expressed through genocidal

tendencies or environmental disasters. Fortunately, this eclipse is not visible from land, which hopefully will reduce its negative impact. Still, it's a reminder to let go of deeply rooted responses, habits, and rituals that tend to alienate individuals and groups from one another.

November 25, Solar Eclipse in Sagittarius:
Twist of Fate
A tense square from muscular Mars to this eclipse can trigger philosophical, political, or religious conflict. Yet even as tensions rise, the possibility for a sudden breakthrough that overcomes long-standing differences is shown by a creative trine to the Sun and Moon from radical Uranus. Visible only in Antarctica, this looks like a chance for humanity to chill some hot spots and invent less destructive ways of expressing contrary points of view.

December 10, Lunar Eclipse in Gemini:
Just Do It
This Lunar Eclipse in chatty Gemini signals a need to stop talking and beating around the bush. It's time to turn words into action with a dynamic square from Mars to this Sun-Moon opposition. Although

it's natural to feel edgy under this influence, the point is to create something new instead of arguing about the same old unresolved issues. It's a chance to become inspired by fresh goals and develop the skills needed to achieve them.

THE BOTTOM LINE:
A CALL TO ACTION

The rate of social change has already increased, and it will continue to get even faster. The media are buzzing about transformational shifts that are supposed to accompany the ending of the Mayan calendar in 2012. Unfortunately, the focus on ancient prophecies overlooks the profound astrological influences that are at play. The incredible planetary forces that began to reshape the future of humanity in the fall of 2008 will reach a crescendo in 2012 when the slow-moving Uranus-Pluto square is exact for the first time. Undoubtedly, major changes will occur during the seven repetitions of this aspect through 2015 that are reawakening the energy of the 1960s when revolutionary Uranus conjoined evolutionary Pluto. Although this square is not exact in 2011, the planets are close enough—within a couple of degrees throughout the summer—to reveal the most significant issues we will be working with for the next several years.

We cannot wait until 2012, for it might be too late then to start the work that so desperately needs to be done now. We are at a rare turning point this year, with the formative forces of Uranus and Jupiter aligning in magical Pisces prior to crossing the threshold and entering Aries, the first sign of the zodiac. Having four out of five of the outermost planets in initiating cardinal signs suggests the opening of a new era. Adding the looming square between reactionary Uranus and metamorphic Pluto underscores the intense level of cultural change we now face.

The system will fall apart unless we rebuild it from the bottom up in a manner that can sustain us into the future. We may be ready to take a quantum leap forward, but it's not going to happen on its own. No one is going to fix things for us. As Native American elders have said, "We are the ones we've been waiting for."

Remember that all of these astrological events are part of the general cosmic weather of the year, but will affect us each differently based upon our individual astrological signs.

GEMINI
AUGUST–DECEMBER
2010 OVERVIEW

SUMMER STORMS

The month opens with a bang when courageous Jupiter in your 11th House of Dreams and Wishes squares ruthless Pluto on **August 3**. You're tempted to do whatever it takes to reach your goals. But ignoring your peers is not a smart idea right now; the tension this could produce isn't worth any success you might achieve. The proud Leo New Moon on **August 9** prompts you to stand up for your beliefs against those who disagree, but it could be challenging to do so effectively when you're caught up in emotional struggles. Expansive Jupiter in your social 11th House opposes restrictive Saturn in your self-expressive 5th House on **August 16**—the second of three such transits that began on **May 23** and finishes on **March 28, 2011**. Your current task is to seek a level of personal creativity that doesn't upset the stability of your local community of friends and associates, but rather contributes to it.

Your key planet, Mercury, is relatively unaspected all month while it visits your 4th House of Roots. Your mind drifts back to childhood memories as you withdraw socially to spend more private time with your family. Mercury's retrograde turn on **August 20** slows your movement even more. It's followed by demanding Saturn's square to Pluto on **August 21**, requiring you to dig even deeper as you reconsider recent decisions about how you balance work with play. Choosing where to concentrate your energy is crucial—even if your current focus needs modification later on. The intuitive Pisces Full Moon on **August 24** falls in your 10th House of Career and can reveal a clear path to the professional recognition you seek.

SUNDAY 1	
MONDAY 2	
TUESDAY 3 ★	Be cautious not to stir up resistance while tackling a project

WEDNESDAY 4 ★	
THURSDAY 5	
FRIDAY 6 ★	You're ready to take another shot at pleasure

SATURDAY 7 ★	
SUNDAY 8 ★	
MONDAY 9 ★ ●	
TUESDAY 10 ★	
WEDNESDAY 11	
THURSDAY 12	
FRIDAY 13 ★	Changes at work that you thought were finalized may resurface

SATURDAY 14 ★	
SUNDAY 15 ★	
MONDAY 16	
TUESDAY 17	
WEDNESDAY 18	
THURSDAY 19	
FRIDAY 20 ★	**SUPER NOVA DAYS** Prepare to hedge your bets and possibly change your mind later

SATURDAY 21 ★	
SUNDAY 22 ★	
MONDAY 23	
TUESDAY 24 ○	
WEDNESDAY 25	
THURSDAY 26	
FRIDAY 27	
SATURDAY 28	
SUNDAY 29	
MONDAY 30	
TUESDAY 31	

★ designates key date

HEART WIDE OPEN

Although the month may start slowly and end with a bit of turbulence, for the most part you enjoy smooth sailing as your long-term plans are falling into place. Messenger Mercury in analytical Virgo is retrograde in your 4th House of Security, requiring that you go back and address any unresolved family issues. These discussions may create discomfort, though, especially if you're just talking in circles about the same old things. But the mentally sharp Virgo New Moon on **September 8** gets you thinking about what happens next, even if you're still recollecting the past. Jupiter is also retrograde and backs into emotional Pisces and your 10th House of Career on **September 9**, connecting your heart with professional aspirations. The emphasis on feelings is confirmed by Venus's entry into powerful Scorpio in your 6th House of Work on **September 8**, followed by aggressive Mars on **September 14**. A few days after Mercury turns direct on **September 12**, you finally begin to feel you're nearing your goals.

Although philosophical Jupiter and radical Uranus are more mental than emotional, their conjunction in spiritual Pisces on **September 18** is a cosmic wake-up call reminding you to move beyond your rational thoughts and into the sometimes illogical world of intuition. This alignment in your public 10th House can shatter mental blocks that previously prevented you from accepting an important opportunity—but only if you're willing to take a risk. The Fall Equinox on **September 22**, followed by the rowdy Aries Full Moon in your futuristic 11th House on **September 23**, can be a turning point. Although there are challenges ahead, you're on your way and there's no turning back.

WEDNESDAY 1

THURSDAY 2

FRIDAY 3 ★ You turn your gaze inward and backward toward your childhood

SATURDAY 4 ★

SUNDAY 5 ★

MONDAY 6

TUESDAY 7

WEDNESDAY 8 ●

THURSDAY 9

FRIDAY 10

SATURDAY 11

SUNDAY 12 ★ SUPER NOVA DAYS Share your needs with someone special

MONDAY 13 ★

TUESDAY 14 ★

WEDNESDAY 15

THURSDAY 16

FRIDAY 17

SATURDAY 18 ★ Your words have great power when they sync with your truth

SUNDAY 19 ★

MONDAY 20 ★

TUESDAY 21 ★ You're tempted to overdo, overcommit, and overindulge

WEDNESDAY 22 ★

THURSDAY 23 ★ ○

FRIDAY 24

SATURDAY 25 ★ Don't suppress your anger, but express yourself kindly

SUNDAY 26

MONDAY 27

TUESDAY 28

WEDNESDAY 29

THURSDAY 30 ★ Accept the consequences of your previous actions with grace

EVERY MINUTE COUNTS

A flurry of activities kicks off this busy month, which brings so much to do that you fear you're neglecting what truly matters. Mental Mercury is quickly moving through new territory and making up for time lost during last month's retrograde. Your remedial work is finished, and Mercury's entry into your 5th House of Play on **October 3** is a welcome relief. However, the indecisive Libra New Moon on **October 7** brings obstacles to romance or otherwise limits your self-expression as Mercury joins Saturn the Tester on **October 8**. Additionally, romantic Venus begins her retrograde phase in your 6th House of Self-Improvement that day, initiating a seven-week period when you can overanalyze love and cool off an otherwise hot relationship.

Your mind-set becomes more serious as Mercury moves into intense Scorpio on **October 20**. The pioneering Aries Full Moon in your futuristic 11th House on **October 22** pushes you forward, but you could lose your sense of direction as wandering Mars squares illusory Neptune, diffusing your plans and confusing your decisions. Nevertheless, you won't likely waffle for long, as the Sun follows Mercury into intense Scorpio on **October 23**, creating a pack of four planets in your 6th House of Health and Work. There's not much room for fun and games, so you should pay attention to what's on your plate and stay focused on your daily routine. Consider taking small steps to improve the quality of your life; don't shake up too much too soon or you'll end up losing ground, rather than making progress. A tense alignment between constrictive Saturn and dispersive Neptune on **October 27** can force you to revisit old doubts once more before moving on.

FRIDAY 1 ★ Stress subsides and creativity flourishes now

SATURDAY 2 ★
SUNDAY 3 ★
MONDAY 4
TUESDAY 5 ★ Move beyond your fear of change and revise your plans

---

WEDNESDAY 6 ★
THURSDAY 7 ★ ●
FRIDAY 8 ★
SATURDAY 9
SUNDAY 10
MONDAY 11
TUESDAY 12
WEDNESDAY 13
THURSDAY 14
FRIDAY 15
SATURDAY 16
SUNDAY 17
MONDAY 18 ★ Set obligations aside and open your mind to a creative process

---

TUESDAY 19 ★
WEDNESDAY 20 ★
THURSDAY 21
FRIDAY 22 ★ ○ SUPER NOVA DAYS You impatience with routine grows

---

SATURDAY 23 ★
SUNDAY 24 ★
MONDAY 25
TUESDAY 26
WEDNESDAY 27
THURSDAY 28
FRIDAY 29
SATURDAY 30
SUNDAY 31

LABOR OF LOVE

Leave the grand gestures and amazing breakthroughs for another month, Gemini. Now that your 6th House of Daily Routines is accentuated, you need to improve what you already have, rather than rushing off to start something new. The fixed Scorpio New Moon on **November 6** falls in your methodical 6th House, reaffirming your need to practice ethical self-restraint. You'll be able to accomplish more than you think if you eliminate emotional distractions and concentrate on the basic necessities of life. Retrograde Venus slips back into your 5th House of Self-Expression on **November 7**, replenishing your pool of creativity. Luckily, with rational Mercury visiting your 6th House until **November 8**, you can focus on accomplishing your tasks without much effort. The Sun remains in your service-oriented 6th House through **November 22**, giving you plenty of time to find your groove and make gradual refinements to your everyday regimen.

Cautionary yellow lights turn to all-clear green when friendly Venus and hopeful Jupiter turn direct on **November 18**. Your chances for pleasure and delight increase through **November 21**, when the sensual Taurus Full Moon falls in your 12th House of Endings. But the completion of one cycle is also the beginning of the next, and if you tie up enough loose ends, the Sun's entry into inspirational Sagittarius on **November 22** frees you to think about the future instead of living in the past. Although the Sun, Mercury, and Mars are all crowded into your 7th House of Partners, suggesting that working with others is your current path to fulfillment, Venus reenters your 6th House on **November 29**, rewarding the small improvements you continue to make on your own.

MONDAY 1	
TUESDAY 2	
WEDNESDAY 3	
THURSDAY 4 ★	Allow yourself to dream of possibilities, but narrow your vision when taking action
FRIDAY 5 ★	
SATURDAY 6 ★ ●	
SUNDAY 7	
MONDAY 8 ★	Involve others in your next big adventure
TUESDAY 9	
WEDNESDAY 10	
THURSDAY 11	
FRIDAY 12	
SATURDAY 13	
SUNDAY 14	
MONDAY 15 ★	Don't be afraid of taking risks
TUESDAY 16 ★	
WEDNESDAY 17	
THURSDAY 18	
FRIDAY 19 ★	**SUPER NOVA DAYS** Take time to burn off excess energy without risking your career
SATURDAY 20 ★	
SUNDAY 21 ★ ○	
MONDAY 22 ★	
TUESDAY 23	
WEDNESDAY 24	
THURSDAY 25	
FRIDAY 26	
SATURDAY 27	
SUNDAY 28	
MONDAY 29	
TUESDAY 30	

UNEXPECTED GIFT

Your ruling planet, Mercury, holds the key to understanding the month that lies before you. The heavenly messenger turns retrograde on **December 10** and remains in trickster mode until **December 30**, putting a challenging spin on your holiday plans. Saying exactly what you mean can minimize most misunderstandings, as Mercury in earthy Capricorn through **December 18** adds sincerity to your words. Then the messenger backs into easygoing Sagittarius, enabling you to let loose and enjoy the festivities of the season. Fortunately you don't need to wait this long to have a good time: The uplifting Sagittarius New Moon on **December 5** plants a seed of intention in your 7th House of Companions, lighting up your month with fun and frivolity. Although industrious Mars reminds you of the hard work ahead as he enters ambitious Capricorn on **December 7**, he also blesses you with the strength and willpower to sustain your high energy during the weeks ahead.

Throughout the month, profound Jupiter and freedom-loving Uranus slowly move toward a mind-expanding conjunction on **January 4, 2011**, in a series that began on **June 8** and recurred on **September 18**. Again you are shaken as new career opportunities change the way you think about your future. The magnitude of this shift is brought into focus by a Full Moon Eclipse in restless Gemini that occurs just hours prior to the Winter Solstice on **December 21**. This powerful pair of planetary events signals the changing of the cosmic guard. A square from electrifying Uranus and buoyant Jupiter energizes this eclipse, suddenly releasing relationship tension, altering your perceptions of the world, or simply pulling you down the rabbit hole to send you on an exciting, if unexpected, adventure.

WEDNESDAY 1 ★ You may get what you want if you state your needs clearly

---

THURSDAY 2 ★

FRIDAY 3 ★

SATURDAY 4

SUNDAY 5 ★ ● Your words have the power to change the inflexible

---

MONDAY 6

TUESDAY 7 ★ Working cooperatively ensures success

WEDNESDAY 8 ★

THURSDAY 9 ★

FRIDAY 10 ★

SATURDAY 11

SUNDAY 12

MONDAY 13

TUESDAY 14

WEDNESDAY 15

THURSDAY 16 ★ **SUPER NOVA DAYS** Don't involve others in a choice you must make for yourself

---

FRIDAY 17 ★

SATURDAY 18 ★

SUNDAY 19 ★

MONDAY 20 ★

TUESDAY 21 ★ ○

WEDNESDAY 22

THURSDAY 23

FRIDAY 24

SATURDAY 25

SUNDAY 26

MONDAY 27

TUESDAY 28

WEDNESDAY 29

THURSDAY 30

FRIDAY 31

2011 HOROSCOPE

GEMINI

MAY 21–JUNE 20

OVERVIEW OF THE YEAR

Your fertile mind is spinning out more ideas than ever this year, and your challenge is to focus your attention on turning the best ones into reality. Saturn's continuing presence in your 5th House of Fun and Games tells you clearly how important it is to manage your output. Saturn doesn't support abstract ramblings and unfulfilled promises; it demands results. The purpose, though, is not to take the pleasure out of life but to teach you to express yourself more skillfully. Masterful Saturn in the 5th House defines a period of creative maturity when you develop your talents in the arts and in the art of living. **Two key elements are purpose and practice, so set goals and work diligently on reaching them.** Whether it's music, design, sales, or dance, this is a time to demonstrate a greater degree of authority. It is not about controlling others; it's about administrating your message with a well-considered plan and well-defined delivery. If you're successful, you'll be rewarded with more self-confidence and an enhanced capacity to bring joy into your life and the lives of those lucky enough to know you.

One source of inspiration this year is a jet-propelled conjunction between visionary Jupiter and innovative Uranus on January 4, the third in a series that first occurred on June 8 and September 18, 2010. This electrifying event in your 10th House of Career is capable of unleashing brilliant insights that alter the path of your professional life. However, on February 25 pressurized Pluto forms a tense square to exorbitant Jupiter, squeezing out the fluff and forcing you to get down to the bottom line. **Cutting out concepts that sound good on paper but fail the test of reality could look like a setback, but it's another reminder to take yourself seriously enough to concentrate on the best and let go of the rest.** If the message isn't clear enough for you then, stern Saturn's opposition to limitless Jupiter makes the point again on March 28. Your tendency to say yes to friends or colleagues may prove more costly than you expect, unless you've budgeted your time and energy carefully enough to meet their needs and still have enough left over for yourself.

Self-management may not be your strong suit, yet you have a major opportunity to develop your organizational skills and personal power. A key event is the New Moon Eclipse in Gemini on June 1, which reminds you to let go of an aspect of your identity that's no longer serving you. Sometimes a Solar Eclipse marks a loss of status or conflict with an authority figure, but this one can be beneficial because it aligns in a harmonious trine with Saturn. **Such support from the planet of order provides a solid foundation for taking your life in a new direction.** This doesn't have to mean dramatic change obvious to others—it's about deepening your sense of inner purpose through a discipline of your own choosing.

MASTER OF YOUR DOMAIN

Well-organized Saturn in your 5th House of Romance shows that this is not a year for "falling" in love but rather a time when you can consciously create the conditions in which love flows more freely. Your head and heart need to work together so that you can define your personal goals and understand what you must do to achieve them. The real magic comes from being in control of your emotions and applying them to fulfill your desires instead of allowing fantasy to take you like the wind. An exception may occur around the Solar Eclipse on November 25, which falls in your 7th House of Partnerships. Insistent Mars and unconventional Uranus form aspects to the eclipse that could shake up your personal life with surprises. Your ability to make sudden adjustments will help you avoid conflict and increase your chances for meaningful connection.

SERVING A HIGHER PURPOSE

Inspirational Neptune stimulates professional dreams in your 10th House of Career April 4–August 4. The planet of spirituality will return to this house on February 3, 2012, for a fourteen-year stay during which your need to gain meaning from your work—rather than just earning income and recognition—will grow. You can become more sensitive to how your job affects the world and how it affects your spirit. If it's something you believe in, your career can soar on the wings of hope. However, if you're stuck in a boring routine, the emotional and physical costs could wear you out. Avoid giving so much at work that you have little left for yourself, and seek other ways to serve your community if your job doesn't fulfill your altruistic calling.

INCOME INNOVATION

Take a more calculating approach to financial matters this year. A Solar Eclipse in your 2nd House of Resources on July 1, connecting with the complex trio of erratic Uranus, stingy Saturn, and exigent Pluto, might turn money matters upside down in a hurry. Uranus signals an unexpected turn of events, yet both Saturn and Pluto can bring rewards if you think boldly but act patiently. You could see a long-term payoff if you can stay calm in a crisis while finding a unique angle for earning more in your current situation or dreaming up a totally new way to make money.

MOVE IT OR LOSE IT

Two eclipses in your 1st House of Physicality suggest that it's time for a significant change of routine this year. The June 1 Solar Eclipse is a New Moon in thoughtful Gemini, an excellent time to start a new diet or exercise program. A conjunction of Venus and Mars in self-indulgent Taurus falling in your 12th House of Secrets tempts you to hide your unhealthy habits. But even if you set aside willpower for a while, the Gemini Full Moon Eclipse on December 10 makes a tense square with active Mars in meticulous Virgo, which can dramatize physical weaknesses. If you want the energy to fully enjoy the festivities, don't wait for the holidays to pass by before you get in shape.

JOYFUL REPAIRS

You often feel that matters involving home and family are so complicated, you have to handle them perfectly to succeed. This desire to do your best is admirable, but it can cut you off from the playful side of your personality. Issues on the home front triggered by Mercury's retrograde period August 2–26 give you a chance to alter this self-defeating pattern. The cycle begins in your domestic 4th House in worrisome Virgo and ends in joyous Leo, reminding you that when you think with your heart, creative solutions arise to even the most complex issues. It's a lesson worth remembering for the rest of your life.

OFF THE MAP

The unusual becomes normal when Uranus, the ruler of your 9th House of Higher Truth, is joined by adventurous Jupiter on January 4. Flashes of insight now excite your hunger to see exotic places. On February 2, the inventive Aquarius New Moon in your visionary 9th House doubles your urge to leave the past behind and explore new and different worlds. Sticking to a conventional education program can be difficult, so look for alternatives that supply the intellectual freedom you seek. Uranus's return to pioneering Aries on March 11 further heats your desire to break out of your boundaries and discover truth solely on your own terms. You may be less willing to follow anyone else's direction while becoming bolder and more brilliant in creating your own.

HEAVEN ON EARTH

Jupiter, the planet of growth, enters stabilizing Taurus and your 12th House of Spirituality on June 4, where it will stay for one year. This is an excellent time to bring your faith down to earth and make it a comfortable part of your daily life. While your mind may be soaring to new heights, your soul finds solace in nature and through a deeper connection to the physical world. Jupiter's creative trines with regenerating Pluto on July 7, October 28, and March 13, 2012, allow you to see a difficult situation from a positive perspective and transform it into an awesome gain.

RICK & JEFF'S TIP FOR THE YEAR
A New You

The ride may be bumpy at times this year,
especially when you have to adapt to surprises
or suddenly turn your mind in a new direction.
Fortunately, you're usually willing to trade the
safety of predictability for the stimulation of new
experiences. Two eclipses in your sign, though,
show that the real changes are more about
you than your circumstances. The mirror of
relationship is one way to begin recognizing your
blind spots. If you apply the same curiosity you
have about the world to yourself, the discoveries
you make will help end unsatisfactory patterns
and enable your talents to flow more freely.

JANUARY

EYES WIDE OPEN

The beginning of this year is an appropriate time to take a serious look at your relationships. On **January 4**, a Solar Eclipse in your 8th House of Intimacy and Shared Resources brings this delicate subject into the spotlight. Setting goals, stating your needs, and committing to do whatever it takes to fulfill them is a tall order, yet failure to look partnership issues squarely in the eye can undermine your alliances. The next few months establish patterns that may last for years, so speaking your truth to a loved one or business associate is worth the inconvenience, whatever it takes. An explosive conjunction between expansive Jupiter and spontaneous Uranus on the same day adds a jolt of electricity that can shock your world. This dynamic aspect tells you to open your mind and leap forward, rather than hunkering down to protect the status quo.

Magnetic Venus attracts more generous people into your life on **January 7**, when she enters enthusiastic Sagittarius and your 7th House of Others. Yet a sobering Sun-Saturn square reminds you that opportunities can be lost now if you don't think clearly and act decisively. Your ruling planet, Mercury, enters orderly Capricorn on **January 13** to reinforce the message that mental maturity and discipline are essential. Nevertheless, energetic Mars's move into unconventional Aquarius and your 9th House of Philosophy on **January 15**, followed by the creative Sun on **January 20**, offers new ideas and inspiration. On **January 22**, Jupiter returns to initiating Aries and your 11th House of Groups, where it contributes to the rising wave of innovation in your life.

KEEP IN MIND THIS MONTH

The best things you receive from other people take time. Don't be in a hurry to grab when patience and trust earn greater satisfaction.

KEY DATES

★ **JANUARY 4**
buried treasure
A rewarding trine from Jupiter and Uranus to valuable Venus in your 6th House of Employment can show you how to access underused assets. Dig deeply within and you'll find the means and motivation to transform a boring situation into a source of satisfaction. The Solar Eclipse in managerial Capricorn indicates that changing your attitude about authority and rules could make the difference between the joy of getting ahead and the frustration of standing still.

★ **JANUARY 7**
conditional fun
Messages are mixed today; popular Venus attracts positive people into your life while dutiful Saturn squares the Sun. The pleasure planet's entry into your 7th House of Relationships favors the fun side of being with others, yet stern Saturn's aspect to the Sun imposes limits on your playtime. Still, this

blend of bubbly openness and responsibility could show you how to expand your heart and mind without losing your common sense.

SUPER NOVA DAYS

★ **JANUARY 10–13**
speed of sound
Your brain is blasted with incredible ideas and a possible overload of information when mental Mercury squares outrageous Uranus on **January 10** and boundless Jupiter on **January 11**. Fortunately, your ability to react quickly to unexpected circumstances is awe-inspiring as enterprising Mars follows with harmonious hookups to Uranus and Jupiter on **January 12–13**. Better yet, your skill in applying these ingenious responses in practical ways is strengthened by Mercury's clever quintile with solid Saturn on **January 12** and entry into results-oriented Capricorn on **January 13**.

★ **JANUARY 18–19**
light beyond the tunnel
Conversations tend to get heavy with a dense Mercury-Pluto conjunction on **January 18**. A

few pointed words can touch a painful nerve
or stir feelings of mistrust. Yet all your deep
thinking is likely to produce a breakthrough
when the Full Moon in Cancer on **January 19** is
favorably aligned with wise Jupiter. The giant
planet's last few days in compassionate Pisces
broaden your perspective and reveal meaning
that can soothe the wounds of hurtful words.

★ **JANUARY 25–27**
build your case
Your brilliant idea on **January 25** might not
have the impact you expect when a Mercury-
Uranus quintile constructs a beautiful model
of reality that makes perfect sense to you.
However, sluggish Saturn turns retrograde
on **January 26** and Mercury forms a square
to it on the **27th**. You may encounter doubters
or, perhaps, have second thoughts about your
own ideas, slamming the brakes on progress.
A reluctant partner may demand more
evidence before supporting your plan; vital
information might be delayed. Time is testing
you, so be patient and do further research to
back up your beliefs.

FEBRUARY

INTUITION VERSUS LOGIC

This mind-expanding month is rich with insights into a brighter future. You can catch glimpses of images before the rest of us—which might even make you a bit of a prophet now. These visions are ideals to aim for rather than realities of the present, and therein lies your challenge. While your intellect can soar above the clouds, the demands of work and money are not about to disappear. Your inclination to step outside the boundaries of rules and routines starts on **February 1**, when independent Mars and rebellious Uranus connect in a spicy semisquare. Three more planets—the Sun, Venus, and Mercury—aspect radical Uranus on **February 2** during the New Moon in Aquarius, Uranus's home sign, turning life upside down with unexpected opportunities and challenging surprises.

Restraint, though, arrives with artful Venus's entry into serious Capricorn and your 8th House of Deep Sharing on **February 4**. Dealing with cautious partners can ground your flights of fancy. The virtue of taking well-measured steps is revealed on **February 9** when Venus joins incisive Pluto, a combination that exposes hidden costs and complications. If fast-moving ideas are spinning out of control, you may hit a wall of resistance. Yet if your strategy is rooted in reason, you may be rewarded with unexpected resources and support. The Full Moon in expressive Leo on **February 18** lights up your 3rd House of Communication with imagination and creativity. However, the Sun's conjunctions throughout the month with Mercury, Mars, and whimsical Neptune spin stories that are strong on fiction and weak on facts. Do your research before making important declarations and take everything you hear with a dash of skepticism.

KEEP IN MIND THIS MONTH

If the gap between where you are and where you want to be is wide, remember that enjoying the journey is as important as reaching your destination.

KEY DATES

SUPER NOVA DAYS

★ **FEBRUARY 1–3**
intellectual awakening
The centerpiece of this enlightening period is the Aquarius New Moon falling in your 9th House of Truth, Travel, and Higher Education on **February 2**. This Sun-Moon conjunction is joined by impatient Mars, pushing you to make your life more interesting. It's an ideal time for planning an eco-adventure or unconventional learning experience. Mercury's shift into Aquarius on **February 3** provides additional motivation for pursuing new concepts and sharing your ideas more globally.

★ **FEBRUARY 5–7**
measured growth
Trust your instincts on **February 5**, when a scintillating sextile between Mercury and Jupiter turns on your intuition, giving you easy access to positive solutions. On **February 6**, rock-solid trines from Saturn to the Sun and Mars strengthen your desire to build enduring

relationships and your commitment to complete creative projects. Still, hard aspects to expectant Jupiter from Venus and the Sun on **February 6** and from Mars on the **7th** can tempt you into overreaching, so maintain self-control and be wary of poor judgment.

★ **FEBRUARY 14–17**
in and out of focus
Valentine's Day starts with a smart Mercury-Saturn trine that anchors you in logic and common sense. On **February 15**, though, mental Mercury's sketchy semisquare with Jupiter can blur your focus with unreliable information. Getting the right data and speaking with precision are especially important on **February 17**, when Mercury semisquares Pluto, the planet that never forgets. What you say and think now can have lasting impact, so monitor the meanderings of your mind and choose your words carefully.

★ **FEBRUARY 20–21**
the audacity of hope
February 20 is an amazing day with a triple conjunction of Mercury, Mars, and Neptune.

This is a mixed salad of rationality and rashness that allows you to justify the most unlikely behavior. Flipping between volatility and vulnerability will produce colorful but confusing conversations, and careless speech can incite inadvertent conflict. You could succumb to a sense of futility as a dream seems to slip away, yet Mercury's entry into imaginative Pisces on **February 21** opens a window of faith—you'll see that all is well even if you can't quite explain why.

★ **FEBRUARY 25**
the slow road to satisfaction
Mercury joins the Sun in your 10th House of Career, connecting your heart and mind to clarify your professional aspirations. A slow square between Jupiter and Pluto, the last in a series that began on **July 25, 2010**, can turn a small disagreement into a major debate. Trying to align your expectations with those of a partner or colleague is difficult—you're tapping into deep fears and strong desires that cannot be resolved overnight.

MARCH

CHANGING SPEEDS

Finding a consistent pace can be difficult this month; several astrological events are driving you to move more quickly while others are bound to slow you down. The Pisces New Moon on **March 4** pours waters of inspiration into your 10th House of Career, motivating you to seek more meaning in your work. Yet maintaining a peaceful attitude may be more important than the specific job you perform. Don't let unrealistic expectations leave you exhausted from doing too much or disappointed by a lack of purpose. Even the simplest tasks take on nobility when you invest the best of yourself in them. Your mind kicks into a higher gear on **March 9**, when Mercury joins electric Uranus and then leaps into spontaneous Aries. This supercharged combination accelerates thinking and spawns original ideas. Uranus returns to Aries on **March 11**, where it tested the waters **May 27–August 13, 2010**, adding even more fuel to the fire you feel inside.

A yellow caution flag goes up when the Full Moon in careful Virgo squares the Moon's Nodes on **March 19**. You might ignore it, though, with the Sun racing into rambunctious Aries the next day, marking the Vernal Equinox, and joining reckless Uranus on **March 21**. However, your ruling planet, Mercury, is slowing down before it turns retrograde on **March 30**, making it difficult to assimilate new information. The need to calm yourself and take a long-term view of things is underscored by Jupiter's opposition to Saturn on **March 28**. The third alignment of these planets—the first two were on **May 23** and **August 16, 2010**—establishes lasting patterns that you shouldn't rush.

KEEP IN MIND THIS MONTH

Spontaneity makes you feel alive, but if you jump the gun right now you may shoot yourself in the foot.

KEY DATES

★ **MARCH 1-2**
watch your mouth
Friendly Venus attracts entertainingly
original colleagues and friends with a sextile
to Uranus and her entry into Aquarius on
March 1. However, your clever comments
can be misunderstood as Mercury skids off
a semisquare with Venus and into traditional
Saturn the next day. Think carefully before
sharing your opinions.

★ **MARCH 9**
sparks fly
Your brain is buzzing with bright ideas—or
maybe it just feels like you drank a gallon of
coffee. In either case, you are itchy, antsy, and
capable of saying or doing just about anything.
The conjunction of your ruling planet,
Mercury, with reactionary Uranus tempts you
tell someone off, especially the slowpokes
who are terrified of anything new or different.
It's your job to light a fire under those around
you, but the trick is to do it with kindness and

originality to encourage change rather than resistance.

★ **MARCH 13–15**
through the eye of the needle
You might get yourself in a bind on **March 13**, when a Mercury-Pluto square can undermine trust unless you handle confidential information carefully. Then, on **March 14**, passive-aggressive Mars in Pisces aspects unyielding Saturn, complicating tasks and slowing down productivity. Still, if you're frustrated or your feelings are hurt, answers arrive on **March 15** that can make sense of this mess. An enthusiastic Mercury-Jupiter conjunction in irrepressible Aries offers you a fresh perspective and the words to express it brilliantly.

★ **MARCH 17–18**
keeping it real
Your imagination flourishes even if you're fuzzy on the facts thanks to a semisquare between detailed Mercury and spacey Neptune on **March 17**. Still, the laws of gravity bring you

down to earth on **March 18** when authoritative Saturn opposes your ruling planet, Mercury. You will be held accountable for every word you say. Silence is better than winging it now, but backing up your statements with data enhances your credibility.

SUPER NOVA DAYS

★ **MARCH 28–30**

wait it out

The Sun in your 11th House of Groups squaring Pluto in your 8th House of Shared Resources can expose weaknesses and areas of discontent on **March 28**. Your frustration might break out in a power struggle or bury itself as resentment, yet neither approach is ideal. The truth is that you may have reached the end of the road with someone; the relationship must radically change or end. However, the bigger the decision, the more time you should take to make it. Mercury's retrograde turn on **March 30** gives you three weeks to dig more deeply before taking a stand.

APRIL

AT YOUR OWN PACE

The contagious excitement of impatient friends
and ambitious colleagues can kick your energy
up to a higher gear as you attempt to match
their intensity. On **April 2**, macho Mars zips into
impetuous Aries and your 11th House of Groups,
where the Aries New Moon falls on **April 3**. A
conjunction between the Sun and exuberant
Jupiter fans the flames of passion on **April 6**.
While all this drive and vision leaves you ready to
put the pedal to the metal, there's more than one
reason to resist. Messenger Mercury, your ruling
planet, is retrograde until **April 23**, which tends
to punish hasty behavior with misunderstandings
and mixed-up data. It's always wise to back off
a little during Mercury's retrograde, because
errors become more common when caution is
thrown to the wind.

Sober Saturn's opposition to the New Moon also
signals the importance of patience; think several
moves ahead now. The Sun sidles into easygoing
Taurus on **April 20**, which favors a more leisurely
pace of activity. But the Bull's ruling planet, Venus,
fires into irrepressible Aries on **April 21** and meets

untamable Uranus the following day to whet your appetite for surprises and spontaneous social events. It's fine to break your patterns and connect with new people in unusual places, as long as it doesn't prevent you from meeting your obligations. Mercury turning direct on **April 23** is normally a time when you can raise anchor and finally start moving ahead. However, Saturn's opposition to the communication planet at this critical time warns you to consider long-term consequences and test the waters before you jump in.

KEEP IN MIND THIS MONTH

Your competitive juices are flowing; but remember, success comes not from comparing yourself with others, but from running your own race.

KEY DATES

★ **APRIL 3**
revolution number nine

You're torn between your own desire to act immediately and the restraining forces of rules, authorities, and reason as today's wild and crazy Mars-Uranus conjunction meets Saturn's opposition to the Sun. However, if you're well prepared and know what you're doing, one of your lightning strikes of brilliance can hit its mark and transform the ways that you work with others.

★ **APRIL 9–11**
perfect aim

Retrograde Mercury joins the Sun on **April 9** and philosophical Jupiter on **April 11**, deepening your self-awareness, enlivening your communications, and enriching your life with meaning. Just be careful not to push your ideas too aggressively during the combative Mars-Pluto square on **April 11**. This is a time when you can influence minds as long as you choose your words carefully—but any lack of

precision is more likely to provoke anger than
awakening.

SUPER NOVA DAYS

★ **APRIL 17-19**
the truth will set you free
The accommodating Libra Full Moon in your
5th House of Self-Expression on **April 17**
puts you in the spotlight, where your desire
to please others may not reflect your real
feelings. Figuring out what you really want
is essential as Mars opposes record keeper
Saturn on **April 18**, potentially locking you
into a decision. An aggressive Mercury-Mars
conjunction on the **19th** also forces you to take
a stand. Still, it's better to take an unpopular
stance that's true to your heart than to
mislead others or lie to yourself just to keep
the peace.

★ **APRIL 22**
risk management
Friends and associates cajole you to take
chances thanks to a thrill-seeking conjunction
of Venus and Uranus in Aries. Your efforts to

keep up with the cool kids, though, may not be worth it. The excitement of a new experience or a fleeting attraction can pass quickly, but losing the trust of someone you respect won't disappear overnight. It's fine to push your boundaries in pursuit of new forms of pleasure—as long as no one, including you, is hurt when you cross the line.

★ **APRIL 27**
a diamond in the rough
A frustrating square between vivacious Venus and compelling Pluto complicates your relationships, especially on the job. Jealous co-workers or an insecure boss may be unwilling to give you the approval you deserve. It doesn't help to complain or go off in a corner and sulk. If you're really dissatisfied, take a deeper look at your abilities and interests. You may have an underused talent that just needs polishing to earn you the rewards you desire.

MAY

TURNING THE CORNER

You are almost ready to begin a new annual cycle, Gemini—but first comes this transitional month, a time to complete unfinished business and let go of the past. It starts with the Taurus Sun in your 12th House of Endings, where you have a chance to reconnect with your spiritual center. The Taurus New Moon in your 12th House on **May 3** nudges you to dive into a limitless pool of faith and imagination. Take time to meditate and commune with nature to quiet your busy mind and align yourself with the divine source of life. Transformative Pluto's trine to the New Moon from your 8th House of Deep Sharing points out where you are supported and also where you're undernourished in relationships. Loyal Saturn's quincunx to the New Moon from your romantic 5th House represents the high price of keeping up appearances with disappointing partners.

You're tempted to retreat from the world when Mars visits your reclusive 12th House on **May 11**, and Venus and Mercury are quick to follow on **May 15**. Intimate conversations and precious moments of self-reflection, however, can reward you with a profound sense of belonging to something larger than yourself. The Scorpio Full Moon on **May 17** rocks the waters of your work-oriented 6th House with pressure to produce more for less money, prompting you to consider changing jobs. On **May 21**, the Sun enters Gemini, illuminating your sign and opening your heart to a fresh world of creative possibilities. Mental Mercury closes the month by taking you on a roller-coaster ride of shifting perspectives with its rapid transition of hard aspects to electrifying Uranus on **May 27** and demanding Pluto and Saturn on the **29th and 31st**.

KEEP IN MIND THIS MONTH

Your most important work—nourishing your soul and revitalizing your spirit—is private. No one else needs to see.

KEY DATES

★ **MAY 1–2**

course correction

Enthusiastic friends encourage you to take
risks or engage in competitive behavior on
May 1, motivated by the firestorm conjunction
of Mars and Jupiter burning in your 11th House
of Groups. Reckless behavior right now could
pull you wildly off course, because a Mercury-
Neptune semisquare suggests misinformation
or a lack of clear thinking. In addition, a stern
Saturn-Sun quincunx on **May 2** will hold you
accountable for inappropriate conduct and
demand immediate adjustments.

★ **MAY 9–11**

motivational speaker

Life can be delightful on **May 9** with a
Mercury-Venus conjunction that serves
up sweet talk and caring conversations,
allowing you to deliver a difficult message
with kindness. And you can charm the birds
right out of the trees on **May 11**, when rational
Mercury joins global Jupiter to open your mind

and expand your horizons. Your passionate words inspire others to take action, making you a leader, whether you seek that role or not. Visions of a more stimulating tomorrow empower you to speak boldly today.

★ **MAY 16**
pillow talk
Convivial Mercury and captivating Venus like each other so much that they join again today for the second time in a week. This time the Moon is in secretive Scorpio, which intensifies discussions and colors flirtations with a sexy undertone. Choose your words wisely, because they can touch others deeply with lasting effects.

SUPER NOVA DAYS

★ **MAY 20-23**
final countdown
You could be purring with power when potent Pluto harmoniously trines a Mercury-Mars conjunction on **May 20**. If you haven't already tossed aside outmoded habits and expectations, purging them now can set you free. Mercury's

alignment with Mars sharpens your tongue and focuses your mind, turning words into action. The Sun's entry into versatile Gemini on **May 21** also gives you a lift that builds your confidence and courage. Take cautious steps on **May 22**, though, as nebulous Neptune's square to the Sun blurs judgment and wastes energy with distractions that could weaken your resolve. Adjust your pace if the Mercury-Saturn quincunx on the **23rd** bogs you down with malcontents when you're ready to fly.

★ **MAY 27–29**
survival of the fittest
Mercury slams into a semisquare with edgy Uranus on **May 27** to send your mind off in strange directions. You may come up with some amazing insights, but for every useful idea, you may have three that won't work. If you don't edit your messages now, you'll have no choice when Mercury clashes with brutal Pluto on the **29th**. Others may shut you down, or you may go through your own mental vetting process to reject concepts that can't pass the reality test.

JUNE

A WHOLE NEW STORY

The transitions that began last month were simply setting the table for the major changes you're facing now. The main player in this story is a Solar Eclipse in Gemini on **June 1**. This supercharged New Moon shines a laser at the core of your being, challenging you to examine your life's purpose and direction. Mercury's entry into versatile Gemini on **June 2** reveals your range of choices. Intellect alone won't answer your most pressing questions, yet a deeper awareness may begin to emerge when visionary Jupiter starts a one-year visit in your 12th House of Soul Consciousness on **June 4**. This wise planet's presence in earthy Taurus is advising to you seek truth in simplicity. An integrating sextile between Jupiter and Neptune on **June 8** signals an opportunity for self-forgiveness and spiritual insights.

Seductive Venus dances into flirty Gemini on **June 9**, and you notice others glancing at you with approval. Yet a Full Moon Eclipse in your 7th House of Relationships on **June 15** is likely to bring out true feelings that can alter the nature of a partnership. It may feel scary to be direct with someone, or for another to be so blunt with you, but it's better to be as honest as you can now than to beat around the bush any longer. If pride is wounded, Mercury's move into tender Cancer on **June 16** softens words and allows you to be more sensitive. On **June 20th**, Mars shoots into your sign, urging you to show more initiative, yet you may have doubts when the Sun enters passive Cancer on **June 21**, marking the Summer Solstice. The Sun's opposition to all-or-nothing Pluto on **June 28** continues the relationship theme, requiring you to stand up for your beliefs, no matter what.

KEEP IN MIND THIS MONTH

Making a fresh start doesn't mean you have to hurry. Study the situation carefully to be sure your next move is the right one.

KEY DATES

SUPER NOVA DAYS

★ **JUNE 1–3**

work in progress

The Solar Eclipse New Moon in Gemini on **June 1** could threaten your current status. Happily, few people are more adaptable than you when change comes along. In fact, if you're bored, you might just shake your own tree to see what happens. Your ruling planet, Mercury, shifts into Gemini on **June 2** to inundate you with information, yet its stressful square to phantasmagoric Neptune the next day can blur your judgment. What you're seeing may not be real, so consider any bright idea as a rough first draft requiring further refinement.

★ **JUNE 7**

reliable source

You have the perfect combination of creativity and common sense today when Mercury trines responsible Saturn. This aspect enhances your ability to organize information and present it with authority. Whether you're trying to address a personal matter or are dealing with a professional issue, you see things clearly and express yourself with enough conviction to earn the trust of others.

★ **JUNE 12–14**
silence is golden
Mercury's conjunction with the Sun on **June 12** adds power to your words, yet the Moon in Scorpio suggests you should hold back and not say everything that comes to your mind. Glib Mercury has a tendency to talk too much, especially with its conjunction to the Moon's South Node on **June 13**. Sharing useless information or listening to everything others have to say is unproductive. The Sun's conjunction with the South Node in Gemini on **June 14** continues to evoke unnecessary chatter and attracts people filled with facts that are devoid of real meaning.

★ **JUNE 16–19**
sixth sense
Feelings grow stronger when Mercury slips into moody Cancer on **June 16** and favorably

aspects expansive Jupiter and dreamy
Neptune on the **17th**. Trust your intuition now,
especially when it comes to finances. You
may not be able to prove your ideas, but what
you sense is worth more than facts. Mercury
tussles with Uranus on **June 18** and with Pluto
on the **19th**, which can shake your faith. Don't
let external pressure or harsh words dislodge
your personal truth.

★ **JUNE 25–26**
  escape hatch
  The Sun in your 2nd House of Resources
  sextiles Jupiter on **June 25** and opens your
  eyes to assets that you haven't yet fully
  exploited. Still, you're probably thinking more
  about getting away from it all than about
  increasing your income. An impetuous Sun-
  Uranus square on **June 26** triggers your
  instinct to rebel against anything or anyone
  holding you down, even if it's against your best
  interests.

JULY

DOLLARS MAKE SENSE

Money muscles its way into the picture this month with plenty of planetary activity in your 2nd House of Income. The most important event is a Solar Eclipse on **July 1** that falls in your 2nd House. Normally, this New Moon in security-conscious Cancer would remind you to manage your cash flow more carefully. This particular lunation, however, is also a powerful eclipse that can radically alter your financial picture. The eclipse sends conflicting messages as it opposes penny-pinching Pluto and squares safety-seeking Saturn and freedom-loving Uranus. If you have a dream of gold and glory and a strategy to make it happen, now's the time to give it serious consideration. If not, it may be wise to develop more conservative spending habits. Magnetic Venus's entry into your 2nd House on **July 4** can tempt your vanity by enticing you to buy the latest fashion or gadget. You may, though, find more value in restoring a cherished object you already own or developing one of your creative talents.

The power of the past reawakens on **July 7** thanks to a Jupiter-Pluto trine that will return on

October 28 and **March 13, 2012**. Forgotten skills and interests may resurface to strengthen your faith and transform a potential loss into a long-term gain. On **July 15**, the constructive Capricorn Full Moon falls in your 8th House of Regeneration, where the guidance of an experienced individual helps you find focus and discipline. Fortunately, there's fun coming your way, too, with the Sun's entry into lively Leo and your 3rd House of Communication on **July 23**. Enthusiastically exchanging ideas with dynamic people is sure to warm your heart.

KEEP IN MIND THIS MONTH

Slow down and seek moderation when managing your money instead of oscillating between reckless spending and worrying about every cent.

KEY DATES

★ **JULY 1-2**
walk your talk
The 2nd House Solar Eclipse on **July 1** may shake your economic base, but you are approaching a reservoir of bright ideas that could save the day. On **July 2**, mischievous Mercury enters courageous Leo and your 3rd House of Information to heat up your communication and add boldness to your message. Mercury's slippery quincunx with Neptune, though, can play fast and loose with facts while a hard-nosed Sun-Saturn square is sure to hold you responsible for any errors.

★ **JULY 8-9**
straight from your heart
Relationships turn dramatic when loving Venus opposes Pluto on **July 8**. If you don't think you're getting your fair share from a partner, express your feelings gently instead of simmering with resentment. When you quiet the demons of fear, you'll remember that giving more will get you more—especially

when magnanimous Jupiter sextiles Venus on **July 9** and your mind is calmed with a mature Mercury-Saturn connection.

★ **JULY 15–16**
up against the wall
The Capricorn Full Moon in your 8th House of Transformation on **July 15** can bring down the hammer of authority. A demanding boss or partner is not in an approving mood, and you're in no mood to listen. Your ruling planet, Mercury, harshly aspects independent Uranus on the **15th** and resistant Pluto on the **16th**, setting you up for verbal conflict. Yet your real struggle right now is in recognizing that limits imposed from the outside might actually be good for you.

★ **JULY 23**
face the music
Celebration of the Sun's entry into proud Leo is tempered by a skeptical semisquare between Mercury and Saturn. An unreliable quincunx between the Sun and fuzzy Neptune leaves you lost in fantasies; you'd be wise to

deal with any doubts, whether your own or those of other people.

SUPER NOVA DAYS

★ **JULY 28–30**

gifts best opened slowly

A joyous heart and a keen intellect are yours when Venus moves into Leo and Mercury enters Virgo on **July 28**. The messenger planet in your 4th House of Roots sharpens your mind. Use your newfound critical thinking to weed out wacky ideas and bring more order to your home life. However, don't be in a hurry to lay down lasting rules as Mercury's opposition to confusing Neptune on **July 29** could prove misleading. Listen without speaking to read Neptune's mysterious messages instead of rushing to put dreams or wounded feelings into words. The New Moon in your objective 3rd House on **July 30** clears mental and emotional palates. Suddenly you can see life with fresh eyes and express yourself with greater confidence.

AUGUST

PRACTICE MAKES PERFECT

The bold Leo Sun burns through your 3rd House of Communication until **August 23**, offering a brightly lit stage for expressing your ideas. You have plentiful opportunities to speak up, but you'd better rehearse your lines carefully to make the most of them. That's because Mercury will be retrograde **August 2–26**, a period when verbal mishaps occur more frequently. Think through any significant discussion—public or private—in advance to make sure that you're on point. Action-planet Mars enters hypersensitive Cancer on **August 3**, undercutting objectivity with feelings. This produces a more delicate environment in which mistakes won't be quickly forgotten or forgiven.

Charm can take you a long way on **August 13**, when the Full Moon in brilliant Aquarius opposes gracious Venus. Normally, this lunation in your opinionated 9th House is a time of mental breakthroughs and intellectual feats of strength. Right now, however, the focus is also on your heart; don't let big ideas get in the way of the small things that show others how much you care.

Dutiful Saturn's squishy sesquisquare with illusory Neptune on **August 24**—the last in a series that began on **October 27, 2010**—confronts you with a choice between the real and the ideal. Still, it doesn't mean that you must discard your dreams or surrender your sense of responsibility. This aspect is a magical lesson in learning how to integrate the worlds of mind and matter. Mercury's direct turn on **August 26** and the competent Virgo New Moon on **August 28** reveal your readiness to develop these new skills.

KEEP IN MIND THIS MONTH

The river of wisdom flows deeply in you, but you may have to stop talking long enough to hear its subtle message.

KEY DATES

★ **AUGUST 2–4**
many shades of gray
Look within yourself for wisdom when
Mercury turns retrograde on **August 2**,
followed by Mars's shift into emotional Cancer
the following day. A slick sextile between
these two planets on **August 4**, though,
promises mental efficiency of a different kind.
Pay attention to the tone of your words right
now, and shade them carefully to express your
underlying feelings. Facts may fail to impress
your audience while sensitive and poetic use of
language conveys more meaning.

★ **AUGUST 8**
dazed and confused
Put down the bank statements and
spreadsheets; numbers are likely to make
you dizzy today. Mercury backs into theatrical
Leo and immediately opposes impressionistic
Neptune, which is great for music, art, and
dance but lousy for taking care of business.
Escaping from reality with fanciful storytelling

is only dangerous if you deny that your mind is in fantasyland. It's wiser to use this time creatively than to try to force clarity.

SUPER NOVA DAYS

★ **AUGUST 13–17**
domino effect
The humanistic Aquarius Full Moon on **August 13** adds social energy useful for planning a party or serving as a peacemaker, especially with so many aspects among Mercury, Venus, Mars, and the Sun over the days ahead. Chatty Mercury, attractive Venus, and the Sun are all conjunct on **August 16**, spurred on by semisquares from Mars through the **17th**. It's easy to become so overloaded with input and activities that the only way to find space is to push others away. Try saying no before you've gone so far that anger seems like the only way out.

★ **AUGUST 21–23**
handle with care
Venus opposes sacrificial Neptune on **August 21** and then enters discriminating Virgo, sending

mixed signals about relationships. A narrowly focused Mercury-Pluto connection on **August 22** urges you to make a decision—yet you'll find resolution elusive given the Sun's aspects to tough Saturn and soft Neptune. The Sun's shift into Virgo on **August 23** touches your 4th House of Roots, reminding you that attending to your own needs is the best way to figure out what to do about others.

★ **AUGUST 24–27**
angel in the wings
On **August 25**, insecure Mars in Cancer in your 2nd House of Money triggers the complex Saturn-Neptune sesquisquare that was exact on the **24th**. You find yourself frustrated over finances and extremely impatient with Mercury's irritable aspect to restless Uranus **August 25–27**. However, a shrewd Venus-Pluto trine helps you to be fiscally and emotionally resourceful. And someone who has been waiting on the sidelines may now be ready to offer you a helping hand after Mercury turns direct on **August 26**.

SEPTEMBER

DUTIES AND DELIGHTS

A delicate dance between work and play demands your attention this month. The Sun in efficient Virgo requires you to do some personal cleanup and reorganization while it occupies your 4th House of Roots until **September 23**. Mercury's move into Virgo on **September 9** focuses your energy on what you need to fix at home and within your family. You're likely to be more self-critical now—but think of it as an opportunity to recognize unhealthy habits clearly enough that you can actually begin changing them. This can be a slow process because you're dealing with deeply rooted patterns that are just beginning to emerge into consciousness. The Full Moon on **September 12** in vulnerable Pisces and your 10th House of Career exposes your insecurities over work. Finding inspiration on the job or in other forms of public service can help to wash away your worries.

The playful side of the equation is emphasized when delightful Venus enters your 5th House of Fun and Games on **September 14**. Mars's shift into affectionate Leo on **September 18** and the Sun's

move into amicable Libra and your 5th House on
September 23 continue to roll out waves of joy.
Confidence, creativity, and even romance can
rise to greater heights when Mercury enters your
entertaining 5th House on **September 25**, followed
by the Libra New Moon on **September 27**. There
may be a price to pay, however, since domineering
Pluto forms a stressful square to the New Moon.
You could be forced to make a difficult choice when
warm Venus joins cold Saturn on **September 29**,
closing one path toward pleasure in order to keep
another one open.

KEEP IN MIND THIS MONTH

*Doing the hard work of addressing your stickiest
personal problems first will make the pleasure that
follows even more delicious.*

KEY DATES

★ SEPTEMBER 8–9
reality stress test

You feel as if you're in an altered state when mental Mercury opposes intoxicating Neptune on **September 8**. Thoughts wander in and out of your head and words wobble in the mists of imagination. Reality strikes hard on **September 9**, though, when Mercury steps into Virgo and precise outlines of objectivity chase away illusions. Strict Saturn's semisquare to Mercury rejects anything that can't be proven. Although this is a tough gauntlet of skepticism that squeezes out weak concepts, the best ideas will profit from the pressure that properly shapes them and brings them down to earth.

SUPER NOVA DAYS
★ SEPTEMBER 12–14
proactive measures

The Pisces Full Moon on **September 12** could put you in a vulnerable situation at your job. If you've been careless in handling a task, you may be held accountable for it now. Yet even if you're on top of your professional game, this lunation in your 10th House of Career may leave you feeling isolated and unsupported with an endless load of work. Instead of withdrawing and feeling wounded, talk to your colleagues about getting the help you need. A perceptive trine between Mercury and Pluto shows you where the resources are and gives you a quiet power of persuasion to bring them over to your side. Even better, a super-smart trine between Mercury and boundless Jupiter reveals the bigger picture on **September 14**— an excellent day for long-range planning and succeeding at office politics.

★ **SEPTEMBER 22–25**
a glimpse of reason
Mercury's tense aspect to exaggerating Jupiter on **September 22** throws off your perceptions. Your confidence is renewed with the Sun's shift into artistic Libra on **September 23**, which is the Autumn Equinox; however Mercury's slippery quincunx with Neptune implies miscommunication the

following day. Inner balance and clarity of thought finally return when Mercury enters objective Libra on the **25th**. Yet even this may be a temporary break in the weather before storms of uncertainty return.

★ **SEPTEMBER 27–28**
know thyself
The lovely Libra New Moon on **September 27** is bright and shiny in your 5th House of Self-Expression. However, the neatly pressed lines of this stylish sign are wrinkled with strange ideas and interruptions. Mercury's opposition to unsettling Uranus on the **27th** could spawn brilliant thoughts, yet it's more likely to keep you on edge. Perhaps you're feeling the drumbeat of the Sun and Mercury's threatening squares with Pluto on **September 28**, which sow seeds of mistrust and secrecy. Obviously you can't control other people's thoughts, but the Mercury-Sun conjunction could bring peace to your own mind.

OCTOBER

THE ART OF REGENERATION

Responsibility forces its stern hand onto your playground this month, interrupting the fun to remind you not to spend time frivolously. The games, distractions, and flirtations that keep your naturally curious mind happily entertained run into walls of resistance on several fronts. Stylish Venus is the first to leave the party when she says good-bye to your lighthearted 5th House on **October 9**. Turn your intensity toward your job, because the love planet then enters Scorpio and your 6th House of Work. Finding a deeper level of motivation and developing your skills could eventually earn you more recognition and fulfillment. On **October 11**, the Full Moon in energizing Aries falls in your 11th House of Groups and Friends, which usually spurs new activity in your social life. However, this one is shadowed by somber Saturn's conjunction to the Sun and opposition to the Moon; elf-doubt or external restrictions may diminish your optimism.

The Sun's move into passionate Scorpio and your 6th House on **October 23** underscores the pressing demands of your daily life. Still, you may see some light at the end of the tunnel on **October 26**, when upbeat Jupiter in your 12th House of Spirituality and Dreams opposes the intense Scorpio New Moon. While others operate in a dog-eat-dog world of limited resources, you may be tapping into a well of boundless faith and imagination that counters their fears. Growth arising from loss is a powerful theme expressed through Jupiter's harmonious trine to transformational Pluto on **October 28**, the second in a series that began on **July 7** and ends on **March 13, 2012**.

KEEP IN MIND THIS MONTH

Taking the easy way out may seem like a shortcut on the road to success, but in the long run it will only slow your progress.

KEY DATES

★ **OCTOBER 6**
get smart

You can make a very strong impression
today if you've planned your presentation
carefully. A Mercury-Saturn conjunction
rewards your discipline with respect but
offers rejection when you shoot from the hip.
Seeing a problem clearly is not an invitation to
despair but a well-drawn map to its solution.
If you're exposed for lacking knowledge
where it counts, don't make excuses. Find the
information you need, commit it to memory,
and others will be suitably impressed.

★ **OCTOBER 11–13**
you first

The impetuous Aries Full Moon on **October 11**
can attract impatient friends or colleagues.
Dynamic Mars's supportive trine tempts
you to try to keep pace, but responsible
Saturn's conjunction to the Sun demands
self-control. This union is exact in your 5th
House of Creativity on **October 13**, reminding

you to follow your own star instead of being distracted by others. Mercury's shift into unwavering Scorpio is another signal to narrow your focus and stick to your priorities. Saying no may not be received well, yet attending to your own needs is a key to maintaining self-respect.

★ **OCTOBER 16–17**
verbal virtuosity
You're especially persuasive on **October 16** with deep ideas and powerful words. Respect this force and avoid diluting your message with too much information. A succinct Mercury-Pluto sextile urges you not to give up until you gather the data you need and find the right language to send a convincing message. On **October 17**, Mercury's opposition to enlightening Jupiter floods you with observations that you can share enthusiastically with others. While channels of communication open wide, be alert to an overdose of optimism that has you promising more than you can deliver or overestimating someone else's contribution.

★ **OCTOBER 23–24**
surprising solution
You're filled with new excitement for your job
thanks to the Sun's entry into your 6th House
of Employment on **October 23**. But you quickly
grow restless and rebellious when Mercury
clashes with rowdy Uranus the next day.
These two threads magically come together
when you apply unconventional ideas to make
your work more interesting.

SUPER NOVA DAYS

★ **OCTOBER 26–28**
the fire of desire
The 6th House Scorpio New Moon opposite
enterprising Jupiter on **October 26** is cooking
up a big idea for your professional life—so big
that it may seem out of reach, yet you'll find
the drive to go for it anyway. Mercury's tense
square with Mars on **October 28** urges you to
stretch yourself, which is a wiser choice than
wasting this force on fighting. And the Jupiter-
Pluto trine opens treasure chests of resources
and rewards when you transform your fear of
having less into passion for getting more.

NOVEMBER

TRAFFIC MANAGEMENT

Your enthusiasm for connecting with people could create problems this month. Vivacious Venus and chatty Mercury enter risk-taking Sagittarius and your 7th House of Others on **November 2**, increasing your opportunities for making new contacts. Personal and business alliances seem especially alluring when potential partners are so optimistic and generous. However, you must turn your attention to domestic issues with Mars's move into your 4th House of Home and Family on **November 10**. The Taurus Full Moon on the same day falls in your 12th House of Escapism, drawing you away from public projects and directing your thoughts to private needs and spiritual matters.

The Sun firing into extroverted Sagittarius and your 7th House on **November 22** puts more wind in your social sails, yet Mercury's retrograde turn on **November 24** sends a very different message. Your ruling planet has been slowing down in advance of this change of direction, which makes it harder to assimilate new data and experiences. You're tempted to overstuff your mind with Mercury in opinionated Sagittarius, leaving lots of loose ends. The usual communication complications of Mercury retrograde, lasting until **December 13**, could be extended this time around. The strongest evidence that something may be amiss in your relationships is the Sagittarius New Moon in your 7th House on **November 25**. This lunation is a Solar Eclipse with hard aspects to Mars, Neptune, and Jupiter—a complex combination warning you not to expect too much of others. Any gains that you make in partnerships now only come if you exercise caution and self-control.

KEEP IN MIND THIS MONTH

Turning down an offer that sounds too good to be true will keep you from exhausting yourself chasing rainbows.

KEY DATES

★ **NOVEMBER 1–3**
spellbound
A Mercury-Neptune square on **November 1** clouds your judgment and could diminish your credibility. The future you're envisioning is really only a rough approximation, so consider it speculative for now. You could be inspired by charming people or cast your spell on others with bewitching Venus and witty Mercury moving into your 7th House on **November 2**. The positive mood engendered by these transits floats balloons of hope that might, alas, just drift away. Fortunately, brilliance arrives with a Mercury-Uranus trine on **November 3** to rapidly reveal which balloons to break and which ones to pursue.

★ **NOVEMBER 10**
body and soul
Mars marches into Virgo and your domestic 4th House on **November 10**, leading to conflict in your home. The sharp critical edge of this aspect isn't about tearing

someone down; its purpose is to cut out the extraneous activities and careless habits that reduce your efficiency. On the other hand, the Full Moon in simplistic Taurus seeks the tranquility of escape in your 12th House of Inner Peace. Ideally, this pair shows you ways to attend to practical matters without losing touch with your soul's deeper needs.

★ **NOVEMBER 16–18**
in the zone
Your intuition is cooking with a magical Mercury-Neptune quintile on **November 16**. You may be able to pluck answers out of the air—as long as you don't overanalyze or let logic get in the way of your instincts. A high-octane trine from energetic Mars to limitless Jupiter provides reserves of power. It's amazing how much you can get done when you maintain a steady pace rather than rushing through your day. Avoid overconfidence on **November 18**, when Jupiter's ungainly sesquisquare with Mercury makes it easy to miss a critical detail. Enthusiasm is terrific

as long as your ideas are anchored in facts as well as faith.

SUPER NOVA DAYS

★ **NOVEMBER 23–25**

quantum leap

You're inspired by someone else's brilliant vision when the Sun trines ingenious Uranus on **November 23**. Reaching this lofty height requires personal discipline, and a determined Mars-Pluto trine can bring you the support of an influential ally. But then Mercury turns retrograde on **November 24** and the Sun is eclipsed on the **25th**. Delays create doubt, and changing partners—or partners changing plans—can feel like major setbacks. Think of this as a thunderstorm that's frightening when it happens but clears the air by the time it's gone. Modifying arrangements with those you rely upon could require weeks of renegotiations but will leave you on more solid ground once the work is done.

DECEMBER

SAY GOOD-BYE TO YESTERDAY

Your year ends, Gemini, with a long look back
that can change your view of the past and reduce
its influence on your life. The key event is a
Lunar Eclipse in Gemini on **December 10** that's
bound to cause some serious soul searching.
You may be tempted to talk your feelings away
instead of facing them, but the message is clear:
Let go of an old story about yourself that keeps
you turning in circles. Mercury is retrograde
until **December 13**, encouraging you to use this
month as a time of review. Pay close attention
to relationship patterns that are tying you up in
knots with this backward cycle in your 7th House
of Partnerships. Mercury's conjunction with your
Sun on **December 4** can plant seeds of inspiration
that let you write a new script for a happier
future.

Tantalizing Venus's entry into innovative
Aquarius and your 9th House of Higher Truth
on **December 20** is a strong magnet pulling
you toward experimentation and away from
the values of your childhood. Travel, education,
or smart strangers can show you a world of

exotic experiences and liberating ideas to satisfy your ever-curious mind. A wise mentor or reliable ally helps you build a foundation to support this new reality when the Sun's entry into ambitious Capricorn and your resource-rich 8th House marks the Winter Solstice on **December 22**. The Capricorn New Moon on **December 24** tests your commitment with its conjunction to Pluto. This tiny but potent planet will show you the price of reaching for higher goals or taking a relationship to the next level. The cost may be great, but the rewards should be even greater.

KEEP IN MIND THIS MONTH

It's better to stretch yourself and take risks than to allow excuses and distractions to keep you from reaching for the stars.

KEY DATES

★ **DECEMBER 1–4**
dueling egos

You could be feeling a little grumpy and underappreciated with a stingy Venus-Pluto conjunction in your 8th House of Shared Resources on **December 1**. And you're unlikely to take your dissatisfaction sitting down on **December 2**, as a stressful square between the Sun and aggressive Mars can trigger anger and spur you into action. Mercury backs over the Sun and squares Mars on **December 4**, which can bring your emotions to a boil. Impatience could lead to harsh words that you may come to regret. It's fine to be fierce and forceful now as long as your clarity of purpose and expression are equal to the sharpness of your speech.

SUPER NOVA DAYS

★ **DECEMBER 10–11**
leap into the fire

December 10 can be a breakthrough day with the Lunar Eclipse in your sign squared by feisty Mars while explosive Uranus turns direct. You could simply feel edgy, perhaps overwhelmed by a million and one things to do in a short space of time. Uncertainty about where you stand with others comes with a hypersensitive Mercury-Venus semisquare on **December 11**, yet you can successfully ride this shock wave if you act decisively. Even if you make a questionable move, you'll create momentum to take your personal life forward. That can't happen if all you have is words and worry.

★ **DECEMBER 13**
dangling conversations
Mercury's forward turn in your 7th House of Others may finally get you back on track to restart interrupted conversations and move ahead with potential new contacts. This cerebral planet is stopping close to a generous trine with ingenious Uranus while the Moon is in vibrant Leo—a combination bound to generate bright ideas and display your wit and humor.

★ **DECEMBER 22**
lucky break
The Sun's entry into Capricorn and your 8th
House of Intimacy is normally a time for
sober reassessment of personal and financial
relationships. This time, though, you're longing
for excitement and ready to toss caution to the
wind thanks to the Sun's trine to opportunistic
Jupiter and square with audacious Uranus. You
could also be surprised by the sudden shift of
attitude of a conservative person who inspires
you to take on bigger challenges in pursuit of
bigger rewards.

★ **DECEMBER 28–29**
divine intervention
Too much information stretches your nerves
when Mercury sesquisquares Jupiter on
December 28. Yet if reason should fail to
provide the information you seek, Mercury's
spiritual quintile with psychic Neptune the
next day can download answers from a higher
dimension.

APPENDIXES

★

2011 MONTH-AT-A-GLANCE
ASTROCALENDAR

★

FAMOUS GEMINIS

★

GEMINI IN LOVE

JANUARY 2011

SATURDAY 1

SUNDAY 2

MONDAY 3

TUESDAY 4 ★ ● Transform a boring situation into a source of satisfaction

WEDNESDAY 5

THURSDAY 6

FRIDAY 7 ★ Expand your heart and mind without losing your common sense

SATURDAY 8

SUNDAY 9

MONDAY 10 ★ **SUPER NOVA DAYS** React quickly to unexpected circumstances

TUESDAY 11 ★

WEDNESDAY 12 ★

THURSDAY 13 ★

FRIDAY 14

SATURDAY 15

SUNDAY 16

MONDAY 17

TUESDAY 18 ★ Soothe the wounds of hurtful words with compassion

WEDNESDAY 19 ★ ○

THURSDAY 20

FRIDAY 21

SATURDAY 22

SUNDAY 23

MONDAY 24

TUESDAY 25 ★ Do further research to back up your beliefs

WEDNESDAY 26 ★

THURSDAY 27 ★

FRIDAY 28

SATURDAY 29

SUNDAY 30

MONDAY 31

TUESDAY 1 ★ **SUPER NOVA DAYS** Pursue new concepts

WEDNESDAY 2 ★ ●

THURSDAY 3 ★

FRIDAY 4

SATURDAY 5 ★ Maintain self-control and be wary of poor judgment

---

SUNDAY 6 ★

MONDAY 7 ★

TUESDAY 8

WEDNESDAY 9

THURSDAY 10

FRIDAY 11

SATURDAY 12

SUNDAY 13

MONDAY 14 ★ Choose your words carefully

TUESDAY 15 ★

WEDNESDAY 16 ★

THURSDAY 17 ★

FRIDAY 18 ○

SATURDAY 19

SUNDAY 20 ★ Careless speech can incite inadvertent conflict

MONDAY 21 ★

TUESDAY 22

WEDNESDAY 23

THURSDAY 24

FRIDAY 25 ★ Strong desires cannot be resolved overnight

SATURDAY 26

SUNDAY 27

MONDAY 28

TUESDAY 1 ★ Think carefully before sharing your opinions

WEDNESDAY 2 ★	
THURSDAY 3	
FRIDAY 4 ●	
SATURDAY 5	
SUNDAY 6	
MONDAY 7	
TUESDAY 8	

WEDNESDAY 9 ★ Encourage change rather than resistance

THURSDAY 10	
FRIDAY 11	
SATURDAY 12	

SUNDAY 13 ★ Handle confidential information carefully

MONDAY 14 ★	
TUESDAY 15 ★	
WEDNESDAY 16	

THURSDAY 17 ★ Backing up your statements enhances your credibility

FRIDAY 18 ★	
SATURDAY 19 ○	
SUNDAY 20	
MONDAY 21	
TUESDAY 22	
WEDNESDAY 23	
THURSDAY 24	
FRIDAY 25	
SATURDAY 26	
SUNDAY 27	

MONDAY 28 ★ **SUPER NOVA DAYS** Take your time before making big decisions

TUESDAY 29 ★	
WEDNESDAY 30 ★	
THURSDAY 31	

FRIDAY 1

SATURDAY 2

SUNDAY 3 ★ ● Preparation can transform how you work with others

MONDAY 4

TUESDAY 5

WEDNESDAY 6

THURSDAY 7

FRIDAY 8

SATURDAY 9 ★ Don't push your ideas too aggressively

SUNDAY 10 ★

MONDAY 11 ★

TUESDAY 12

WEDNESDAY 13

THURSDAY 14

FRIDAY 15

SATURDAY 16

SUNDAY 17 ★ ○ SUPER NOVA DAYS Stay true to your heart

MONDAY 18 ★

TUESDAY 19 ★

WEDNESDAY 20

THURSDAY 21

FRIDAY 22 ★ Push boundaries but don't cross lines of trust

SATURDAY 23

SUNDAY 24

MONDAY 25

TUESDAY 26

WEDNESDAY 27 ★ Polish an underused talent to earn the rewards you desire

THURSDAY 28

FRIDAY 29

SATURDAY 30

SUNDAY 1 ★ Take risks while being accountable for your actions

MONDAY 2 ★

TUESDAY 3 ●

WEDNESDAY 4

THURSDAY 5

FRIDAY 6

SATURDAY 7

SUNDAY 8

MONDAY 9 ★ Be passionate and inspire others to take action

TUESDAY 10 ★

WEDNESDAY 11 ★

THURSDAY 12

FRIDAY 13

SATURDAY 14

SUNDAY 15

MONDAY 16 ★ Your words can touch others deeply with lasting impact

TUESDAY 17 ○

WEDNESDAY 18

THURSDAY 19

FRIDAY 20 ★ **SUPER NOVA DAYS** Set aside outmoded habits and expectations

SATURDAY 21 ★

SUNDAY 22 ★

MONDAY 23 ★

TUESDAY 24

WEDNESDAY 25

THURSDAY 26

FRIDAY 27 ★ Reject concepts that can't pass the reality test

SATURDAY 28 ★

SUNDAY 29 ★

MONDAY 30

TUESDAY 31

WEDNESDAY 1 ★ ● SUPER NOVA DAYS Bright ideas still need refinement

THURSDAY 2 ★

FRIDAY 3 ★

SATURDAY 4

SUNDAY 5

MONDAY 6

TUESDAY 7 ★ Organize information and present it with authority

WEDNESDAY 8

THURSDAY 9

FRIDAY 10

SATURDAY 11

SUNDAY 12 ★ Don't say everything that comes to your mind

MONDAY 13 ★

TUESDAY 14 ★

WEDNESDAY 15 ○

THURSDAY 16 ★ What you sense is worth more than facts

FRIDAY 17 ★

SATURDAY 18 ★

SUNDAY 19 ★

MONDAY 20

TUESDAY 21

WEDNESDAY 22

THURSDAY 23

FRIDAY 24

SATURDAY 25 ★ Being a rebel may be against your best interests

SUNDAY 26 ★

MONDAY 27

TUESDAY 28

WEDNESDAY 29

THURSDAY 30

FRIDAY 1 ★ ● A reservoir of bright ideas could save the day

SATURDAY 2 ★

SUNDAY 3

MONDAY 4

TUESDAY 5

WEDNESDAY 6

THURSDAY 7

FRIDAY 8 ★ Relationships turn dramatic

SATURDAY 9 ★

SUNDAY 10

MONDAY 11

TUESDAY 12

WEDNESDAY 13

THURSDAY 14

FRIDAY 15 ★ ○ Recognize the limits that are imposed from the outside

SATURDAY 16 ★

SUNDAY 17

MONDAY 18

TUESDAY 19

WEDNESDAY 20

THURSDAY 21

FRIDAY 22

SATURDAY 23 ★ Deal with your doubts if you are lost in fantasies

SUNDAY 24

MONDAY 25

TUESDAY 26

WEDNESDAY 27

THURSDAY 28 ★ **SUPER NOVA DAYS** A joyous heart and a keen intellect are yours

FRIDAY 29 ★

SATURDAY 30 ★ ●

SUNDAY 31

MONDAY 1

TUESDAY 2 ★ Pay attention to the tone of your words

WEDNESDAY 3 ★

THURSDAY 4 ★

FRIDAY 5

SATURDAY 6

SUNDAY 7

MONDAY 8 ★ Use this time creatively instead of forcing clarity

TUESDAY 9

WEDNESDAY 10

THURSDAY 11

FRIDAY 12

SATURDAY 13 ★ ○ SUPER NOVA DAYS Try saying no before going too far

SUNDAY 14 ★

MONDAY 15 ★

TUESDAY 16 ★

WEDNESDAY 17 ★

THURSDAY 18

FRIDAY 19

SATURDAY 20

SUNDAY 21 ★ Attend to your own needs before those of others

MONDAY 22 ★

TUESDAY 23 ★

WEDNESDAY 24 ★ Financial frustration leads to being fiscally resourceful

THURSDAY 25 ★

FRIDAY 26 ★

SATURDAY 27 ★

SUNDAY 28 ●

MONDAY 29

TUESDAY 30

WEDNESDAY 31

THURSDAY 1	
FRIDAY 2	
SATURDAY 3	
SUNDAY 4	
MONDAY 5	
TUESDAY 6	
WEDNESDAY 7	
THURSDAY 8 ★	Objectivity chases away illusions
FRIDAY 9 ★	
SATURDAY 10	
SUNDAY 11	
MONDAY 12 ★	○ SUPER NOVA DAYS Ask your colleagues for help
TUESDAY 13 ★	
WEDNESDAY 14 ★	
THURSDAY 15	
FRIDAY 16	
SATURDAY 17	
SUNDAY 18	
MONDAY 19	
TUESDAY 20	
WEDNESDAY 21	
THURSDAY 22 ★	Mixed messages throw off your perceptions
FRIDAY 23 ★	
SATURDAY 24 ★	
SUNDAY 25 ★	
MONDAY 26	
TUESDAY 27 ★	● You can't control other people's thoughts
WEDNESDAY 28 ★	
THURSDAY 29	
FRIDAY 30	

SATURDAY 1	
SUNDAY 2	
MONDAY 3	
TUESDAY 4	
WEDNESDAY 5	
THURSDAY 6 ★	Find the information you need and commit it to memory
FRIDAY 7	
SATURDAY 8	
SUNDAY 9	
MONDAY 10	
TUESDAY 11 ★	O Follow your own star
WEDNESDAY 12 ★	
THURSDAY 13 ★	
FRIDAY 14	
SATURDAY 15	
SUNDAY 16 ★	Be alert to an overdose of optimism
MONDAY 17 ★	
TUESDAY 18	
WEDNESDAY 19	
THURSDAY 20	
FRIDAY 21	
SATURDAY 22	
SUNDAY 23 ★	Apply unconventional ideas to your work
MONDAY 24 ★	
TUESDAY 25	
WEDNESDAY 26 ★	● **SUPER NOVA DAYS** Transform your fear into passion
THURSDAY 27 ★	
FRIDAY 28 ★	
SATURDAY 29	
SUNDAY 30	
MONDAY 31	

TUESDAY 1 ★ Your dreams can inspire others

WEDNESDAY 2 ★

THURSDAY 3 ★

FRIDAY 4

SATURDAY 5

SUNDAY 6

MONDAY 7

TUESDAY 8

WEDNESDAY 9

THURSDAY 10 ★ ○ Be practical without losing touch with your soul's needs

---

FRIDAY 11

SATURDAY 12

SUNDAY 13

MONDAY 14

TUESDAY 15

WEDNESDAY 16 ★ Don't let logic get in the way of your instincts

---

THURSDAY 17 ★

FRIDAY 18 ★

SATURDAY 19

SUNDAY 20

MONDAY 21

TUESDAY 22

WEDNESDAY 23 ★ SUPER NOVA DAYS Delays can feel like major setbacks

---

THURSDAY 24 ★

FRIDAY 25 ★ ●

SATURDAY 26

SUNDAY 27

MONDAY 28

TUESDAY 29

WEDNESDAY 30

THURSDAY 1 ★ Impatience could lead to harsh words

FRIDAY 2 ★
SATURDAY 3 ★
SUNDAY 4 ★
MONDAY 5
TUESDAY 6
WEDNESDAY 7
THURSDAY 8
FRIDAY 9
SATURDAY 10 ★ ○ **SUPER NOVA DAYS** Acting decisively creates momentum

SUNDAY 11 ★
MONDAY 12
TUESDAY 13 ★ Move ahead with potential new contacts

WEDNESDAY 14
THURSDAY 15
FRIDAY 16
SATURDAY 17
SUNDAY 18
MONDAY 19
TUESDAY 20
WEDNESDAY 21
THURSDAY 22 ★ Toss caution to the wind

FRIDAY 23
SATURDAY 24 ●
SUNDAY 25
MONDAY 26
TUESDAY 27
WEDNESDAY 28 ★ Too much information stretches your nerves

THURSDAY 29 ★
FRIDAY 30
SATURDAY 31

FAMOUS GEMINIS

Mr. T	★	5/21/1952
Notorious B.I.G.	★	5/21/1972
Al Franken	★	5/21/1951
Sir Arthur Conan Doyle	★	5/22/1859
Sir Laurence Olivier	★	5/22/1907
Joan Collins	★	5/23/1933
Bob Dylan	★	5/24/1941
Ralph Waldo Emerson	★	5/25/1803
Lauryn Hill	★	5/25/1975
John Wayne	★	5/26/1907
Stevie Nicks	★	5/26/1948
Pam Grier	★	5/26/1949
Lenny Kravitz	★	5/26/1964
Dashiell Hammett	★	5/27/1894
Vincent Price	★	5/27/1911
Rudolph Giuliani	★	5/28/1944
Kylie Minogue	★	5/28/1968
Patrick Henry	★	5/29/1736
Bob Hope	★	5/29/1903
John F. Kennedy	★	5/29/1917
Melissa Etheridge	★	5/29/1961
Wynonna Judd	★	5/30/1964
Walt Whitman	★	5/31/1819
Clint Eastwood	★	5/31/1930
Brooke Shields	★	5/31/1965
Colin Farrell	★	5/31/1976
Marilyn Monroe	★	6/1/1926
Morgan Freeman	★	6/1/1937
Alanis Morissette	★	6/1/1974
Josephine Baker	★	6/3/1906
Tony Curtis	★	6/3/1925
Allen Ginsberg	★	6/3/1926
Curtis Mayfield	★	6/3/1942
Dr. Ruth Westheimer	★	6/4/1928
Angelina Jolie	★	6/4/1975
Dean Martin	★	6/7/1917
Allen Iverson	★	6/7/1975

FAMOUS GEMINIS

Anna Kournikova	★	6/7/1981
Prince	★	6/7/1958
Frank Lloyd Wright	★	6/8/1867
Barbara Bush	★	6/8/1925
Nancy Sinatra	★	6/8/1940
Cole Porter	★	6/9/1891
Les Paul	★	6/9/1915
Johnny Depp	★	6/9/1963
Michael J. Fox	★	6/9/1961
Judy Garland	★	6/10/1922
Maurice Sendak	★	6/10/1928
Jacques Cousteau	★	6/11/1910
Joe Montana	★	6/11/1956
George H. W. Bush	★	6/12/1924
Anne Frank	★	6/12/1929
William Butler Yeats	★	6/13/1865
Mary-Kate and Ashley Olsen	★	6/13/1986
Harriet Beecher Stowe	★	6/14/1811
Donald Trump	★	6/14/1946
Boy George	★	6/14/1961
Helen Hunt	★	6/15/1963
Ice Cube	★	6/15/1969
Joyce Carol Oates	★	6/16/1938
Tupac Shakur	★	6/16/1971
Igor Stravinsky	★	6/17/1882
M. C. Escher	★	6/17/1898
Newt Gingrich	★	6/17/1943
Venus Williams	★	6/17/1980
Roger Ebert	★	6/18/1942
Paul McCartney	★	6/18/1942
Lou Gehrig	★	6/19/1903
Salman Rushdie	★	6/19/1947
Paula Abdul	★	6/19/1962
Lionel Richie	★	6/20/1949
Nicole Kidman	★	6/20/1967

GEMINI IN LOVE

GEMINI & ARIES (MARCH 21–APRIL 19)

Your spontaneity mixes well with action-oriented Aries, making a lighthearted and congenial couple. You both usually choose to experience the brighter side of life. Together you contribute your share of joy to the world around you. Communication is very important to you, and in many ways you actually express your love through ideas and the words used to share them. Your Aries lover, on the other hand, is less inclined to intellectualism and is more tactile and immediate. He or she will need some independence and your comings and goings should provide them with enough freedom so that they don't feel too constrained by the demands of the relationship. Will this one last? It's hard to tell, but one thing is certain. You're going to have to make things feel new and exciting for your Aries to stay interested. If your love planet, Venus, is in Aries, then this won't be a problem. It may take some effort to create long-term stability, but you and your Aries friend can inspire each other to invent new and potent ways to express ideas and to lead the way toward a life that you both can enjoy.

GEMINI & TAURUS (APRIL 20–MAY 20)

Your lighthearted and fast-moving mind finds solid ground to rest upon when you team up with a more practical and levelheaded Taurus. The problem is that you may quickly become bored, unless your Moon is in an earth sign (Taurus, Virgo, or Capricorn) or your Mercury is in Taurus. Regardless of other planetary locations, your fast reflexes and agile constitution are quite different from Taurus's slowly deliberate and determined manner. If you can get past your differences in style, the two of you can really enjoy the company of one another. Your mate puts you at rest and allows you to stop spinning your wheels, which lets you make better use of your creative potential. Your brilliant abilities flourish as you put your ideas into a solid format that can be shared with others and built upon. On the other hand, you are the sales person who can promote the Taurus's fine reputation and solid integrity. Although your flirtatious nature may irritate your lover, he or she will stand by you through thick and thin, as long as you don't overdo it.

GEMINI & GEMINI (MAY 21–JUNE 20)

For the most part, people who share the same sun sign have a tremendous amount in common. However, some of the duo sun-sign combinations share their traits more harmoniously than others do. As an air Gemini whose restless mind is always moving, you tend to clash a bit more with a fellow Gemini than other duos. You are such a mercurial chatterbox that in an intimate relationship with another Twin, you may be so busy conjuring clever responses before the other has finished a sentence that you don't really listen to what your equally talkative partner is saying. Obviously, this can cause problems and may create agitation. If you each have your Moon in a water or earth sign, there's a higher level of compatibility and an easy way beyond this problem. No matter what sign your Moon is in, if you learn to focus on your partner rather than just listening to yourself talk, you can dynamically raise each other to new heights. Remember, this relationship is a mental one, and the sexual attraction here is based on the mutual appreciation of the words you share. Together you can be all talk and no action unless you make a real effort to take care of the practical things in your life.

GEMINI & CANCER (JUNE 21–JULY 22)

You are attracted to movement and change. You love parties, meetings, and social engagements—anything where you get to share ideas and exchange words with like-minded people. Your Cancer lover, on the other hand, is not so driven by a need to interact with others. He or she is more attracted to security and home-centered activities, finding satisfaction from nurturing family and loved ones. Your hard-shelled partner is a tenacious Crab and won't easily let go of the past, while you're ready for whatever the present may bring. It boils down to the fact that your Cancer amour is an emotional water sign and you live in airy mental realms, making for different priorities in your everyday lives. However, if your Venus is in Taurus or Cancer, you'll easily appreciate your partner's stay-at-home attitude. Wherever your other planets are, it's essential for you to learn the value of emotional expression, even if it makes you uncomfortable. If you can slow down and let your feelings catch up with your thoughts, your sensitive Cancer friend will add meaning and richness to your life. Ultimately, the two of you find compatibility only if you can find a balance between your feelings and your thoughts.

GEMINI & LEO (JULY 23–AUGUST 22)

Let's face it: you love to flirt and play. The good news is that your Leo mate loves to be flirted with and adored. The playful Lion is usually ready for a good time, but will separate work and play more than you do. If you can find a way to bring lighthearted fun into your time together, you can be highly compatible. Your habit of looking over the fence for greener pastures will not bode well with the possessive Leo, who needs to be the center of your world, along with plenty of immediate attention and applause. You'll have to beware not to hurt your proud Lion's feelings by flaunting interest elsewhere, or your Leo will retreat. If your Venus is in Leo, this may not be a problem. On the upside, your partner will always communicate through his or her heart with generosity and love. There aren't many things better than being loved by a Leo when they are bestowing their grace upon you. Your keen mental wit is attractive to Leo, but your sarcasm may be too much at times. The long-term possibilities may rest on your willingness to learn the virtues of loving communication.

GEMINI & VIRGO (AUGUST 23–SEPT. 22)

With Virgo, you may have found your mental match. This can be good news or bad news, for your thinking styles are very different from one another. Both of you are ruled by the planet Mercury, which governs the mental aspects of the personality, creating quite an analytical and heady relationship. Whereas you are openly expressive and as curious as any cat, your Virgo partner may see you as a bit scattered within your daily focus—or lack of it. If Mercury or Venus is in Taurus in your chart, however, you'll be more focused and compatibility will be much easier. No matter where your other planets are, Virgo can be impatient with you. Meanwhile, you will probably get annoyed by the nitpicky attitudes of your Virgo mate. His or her personality can be somewhat critical, focusing too much on minute details that you think are irrelevant. Harmonious activities that you can share involve reading and discussing books, writing projects, movies, puzzles, and talking about politics or other intellectual topics. You both appreciate the virtue of intelligence— romantic interplay involves wit and candor.

GEMINI & LIBRA (SEPT. 23–OCT. 22)

This is usually a very good combination, for both you and your Libran love are refined and socially aware. Although you may be a little faster with the clever reply, your partner brings a highly developed sense of grace and style that you can incorporate into your everyday life. Creativity is important to you, and this relationship offers the possibility of working together in the visual arts, writing, or music. You can admire each other's taste in food, clothing, and home decorating, although you tend to have more variety than your color-conscious partner. A shared living space works well and would probably include many beautiful books in an atmosphere of sophistication and harmony. Together, you synchronize your energies into a symphony of beauty, through words and images. Of course, individual relationships are more complex than simple sun signs, and your individual Moon signs can create emotional tensions, depending upon their position. Since you both love to entertain, this relationship offers much to your friends and family. In fact, your ultimate compatibility may depend upon sharing your social life, and in doing so, you can shine together in many ways.

GEMINI & SCORPIO (OCT. 23–NOV. 21)

Have you ever thought about ice-skating on hot lava? You like to glide over the surface without much resistance. On the other hand, your Scorpio lover needs the depth of passion. Unless your Moon is in Scorpio or another water sign, you'd prefer to treat passion intellectually rather than physically. Regardless, it's very important for this relationship to be given time to grow. At first impression, your Scorpio will think that you're superficial and perhaps even shallow. The truth is that without Venus or Mars in a water sign, you may not be able or willing to fulfill your lover's need for intense feelings and focused attention. Scorpio may be attracted to your quick wit and cleverness, which will give you time to show your deeper stuff. At first, you may feel exposed by the deeply intimate approach of your Scorpio partner, but in time, you can find an attractive meeting place in mental and physical attraction. Sexy Scorpio explores new ways to involve you in passionate interplay, and your flirtatiousness responds to the depth of Scorpio's interest with sensual and playful charm and charisma. Even if you can't make it last forever, you can experience the intensity of a great love affair.

GEMINI & SAGITTARIUS (NOV. 22–DEC. 21)

You like movement in your life, in your mind, and in your relationships. Your natural curiosity cannot be squelched. With a Sagittarius, you meet someone who is also interested in activity, but the Archer's arrow tends to aim far—Sagittarians are attracted to long journeys rather than lots of little trips. You are most compatible with your Sagittarius within the context of travel and adventure. He or she will share your restlessness, and together you're on the move. If your individual charts are incompatible in Mars, you may have difficulty finding common ground for your adventures. With Sagittarius, you find it easy to be open-minded, and the Archer's global awareness is exciting to you. Together you could plan a climbing expedition or a biking trip across southern France. The two of you can keep each other well occupied with good humor and intelligent conversation. This relationship is good for you as your Sagittarian lover tends to bring out the optimistic side of your life. Together, you can create a cheerful and bright home life. You two are quite compatible and can have a lasting and satisfying relationship for many years, although it may not ever feel fully stable.

GEMINI & CAPRICORN (DEC. 22–JAN. 19)

You are the quick-change artist known for your restless mind and clever wit. Your Capricorn lover is steady, conservative, and not inclined toward light cocktail-party banter. Gemini's character is very different from the Goat's. Whereas you're playful and childlike, searching for ways to communicate ideas with others, your Goat is serious and hardworking, preferring to focus on tasks and goals. Bridging the gap between these two can be extremely rewarding. Your role in the relationship is to help your Capricorn lighten up the load of daily life with your usual upbeat enthusiasm. Meanwhile, your partner can bring steadfast organization into your life. If Venus or Mars in your chart is compatible with your Capricorn lover's chart, then you'll be more open to creating a strong foundation between the two of you. Quiet Capricorn may need to give plenty of attention to talkative Gemini, learning to appreciate candor as well as a playful approach to communication. It will probably be easier for you to allow for the diverse qualities in each other, but if your Goat can loosen up, it's possible for the two of you to join forces, creating a productive relationship with plenty of room for growth and mutual respect.

GEMINI & AQUARIUS (JAN. 20–FEB. 18)

You love to talk about almost anything, and probably know a little bit about practically everything in the world. Your Aquarian lover, however, may know everything. So, although the two of you can have a wonderful intellectual rapport, your styles are different. You're more flexible. Your Aquarian mate can be rather rigid. Nonetheless, you like being with your partner, and never tire of the repartee. Ultimately, you're compatible with Aquarius and can create strong bonds that make you the very best of friends. You are usually willing to engage in fun and entertaining activities, and your Aquarius partner is a great comrade who is willing and ready to try pretty much anything new and different. You have a persuasive effect on Aquarius and may try to talk him or her into delving into previously unexplored avenues. Together, your agile minds prefer to widen the vision by engaging in such topics as space, sci-fi, or anything unusual and intellectually stimulating. This is an enduring platonic union that can turn into love if the chemistry is right. It will probably take strong connections between Venus and Mars in your compatibility charts for the relationship to develop in the physical and romantic realms.

GEMINI & PISCES (FEB. 19–MARCH 20)

You can tap dance your way through clever conversations as if life was an ongoing cocktail party. Your Pisces lover, however, prefers a quiet world of spiritual thought, exotic imagination, and vivid fantasy. While you push forward into the world with confidence and versatility, your partner gently leans into new experiences with uncertainty and sensitive compassion. You have to speak outwardly whereas Pisces requires time to reflect inwardly. As each of you brings a unique personality into this relationship, you will both need to adapt a flexible approach to life. Flexibility is your middle name, but your partner may be difficult for you to read, so you won't know which way to turn. If you have strong contacts between the Moons in your individual charts, you will be more sensitive to each other's needs. Your Fish can teach you how to weave magic and words into ideas with a new awareness and sensitivity. Meanwhile, you encourage Pisces to rise above the water and peek out at a diverse world, helping him or her discover new vistas of experience and fulfillment. A mutually satisfying relationship develops as you each adapt to the different approach the other carries through life.

ABOUT THE AUTHORS

RICK LEVINE When I first encountered astrology as a psychology undergraduate in the late 1960s, I became fascinated with the varieties of human experience. Even now, I love the one-on-one work of seeing clients and looking at their lives through the cosmic lens. But I also love history and utilize astrology to better understand the longer-term cycles of cultural change. My recent DVD, Quantum Astrology, explores some of these transpersonal interests. As a scientist, I'm always looking for patterns in order to improve my ability to predict the outcome of any experiment; as an artist, I'm entranced by the mystery of what we do not and cannot know. As an astrologer, I am privileged to live in an enchanted world that links the rational and magical, physical and spiritual—and yes—even science and art.

JEFF JAWER I'm a Taurus with a Scorpio Moon and Aries rising who lives in the Pacific Northwest with Danick, my double-Pisces musician wife, our two Leo daughters, a black Gemini cat, and a white Pisces dog. I have been a professional astrologer since 1973 when I was a student at the University of Massachusetts (Amherst). I encountered astrology as my first marriage was ending and I was searching for answers. Astrology provided them. More than thirty-five years later, it remains the creative passion of my life as I continue to counsel, write, study, and share ideas with clients and colleagues around the world.

ACKNOWLEDGMENTS

Thanks to Paul O'Brien, our agent, our friend, and the creative genius behind Tarot.com; Gail Goldberg, the editor who always makes us sound better; Marcus Leaver and Michael Fragnito at Sterling Publishing, for their tireless support for the project; Barbara Berger, our supervising editor, who has shepherded this book with Taurean persistence and Aquarian invention; Laura Jorstad, for her refinement of the text; and Sterling project editor Mary Hern, assistant editor Melanie Madden, and designer Gavin Motnyk for their invaluable help. We thank Bob Wietrak and Jules Herbert at Barnes & Noble, and all of the helping hands at Sterling. Thanks for the art and ideas from Jessica Abel and the rest of the Tarot.com team. Thanks as well to 3+Co. for the original design and to Tara Gimmer for the author photo.